MathFlare

Name: ______________________

Class: ___________

Teacher: ______________________

Introduction

As parents and educators, we recognize the pivotal role mathematics plays in shaping a child's academic journey and future success. Yet, the path to mathematical proficiency can often seem daunting, fraught with challenges and complexities. That's where the transformative power of MathFlare Workbooks shine through, illuminating the way forward with clarity, precision, and purpose.

Introducing MathFlare Workbooks – a beacon of guidance, a testament to excellence, and a catalyst for achievement. Crafted with meticulous care and expertise, MathFlare Workbooks stand as paragons of educational excellence, designed to nurture young minds, ignite a passion for learning, and develop a deep-rooted understanding of mathematical concepts.

Picture this: your child eagerly delves into the pages of Mathflare Workbook, greeted by a step-by-step guide illuminated with vivid examples that demystify complex mathematical concepts. With each turn of the page, they embark on a journey of discovery, encountering thoughtfully curated practice questions that reinforce learning and hone problem-solving skills. And when they unveil the answers to those very questions, a sense of accomplishment blossoms within them – a tangible reward for their hard work and dedication.

But MathFlare Workbooks are more than just tools for learning; they are pathways to comprehension, fostering a deep-seated understanding of mathematical concepts through a sequential, logical flow. From fundamental principles to advanced problem-solving strategies, every chapter builds upon the last, ensuring a robust foundation upon which future knowledge can be constructed.

As parents, we yearn for nothing more than to see our children thrive, to witness the spark of inspiration ignited within them as they conquer academic challenges with confidence and poise. MathFlare Workbooks serve as partners in this noble endeavor, offering not just practice questions, but the keys to unlocking a world of opportunity.

And for teachers, MathFlare Workbooks stand as invaluable allies in the quest to cultivate mathematical proficiency in the classroom. With answers readily available, instructors can focus on guiding and nurturing their students, confident in the knowledge that MathFlare Workbooks provide a solid framework upon which to build.

In the pages of MathFlare Workbooks, we find not just the promise of academic excellence, but the seeds of a brighter tomorrow. So let us embrace the power of mathematics, let us champion the journey of learning, and let us pave the way for a generation of young minds poised to shape the world. With MathFlare Workbooks as our guide, the possibilities are infinite, and the future, bright.

Table of Contents

MathFlare
MATH WORKBOOK
Grade 2
Step by Step Guide and Essential Practice with Answers
Addition Subtraction
Multiplication
Place Value and Expanded Notations
Geometry
MathFlare Publishing

MathFlare
MATH WORKBOOK
Grade 2-3
Step by Step Guide and Essential Practice with Answers
Addition Subtraction
Multiplication and Division
Place Value and Expanded Notations
Geometry
MathFlare Publishing

MathFlare
MATH WORKBOOK
Grade 3
Step by Step Guide and Essential Practice with Answers
Multiplication and Division
Decimals
Place Value and Expanded Notations
Fractions and Geometry
MathFlare Publishing

MathFlare
MATH WORKBOOK
Grade 1
Step by Step Guide and Essential Practice with Answers
Counting and Numbers
Addition and Subtraction
Place Value and Expanded Notations
Understanding Time
MathFlare Publishing

MathFlare
MATH WORKBOOK
Grade 1-2
Step by Step Guide and Essential Practice with Answers
Counting and Numbers
Addition and Subtraction
Place Value and Expanded Notations
Understanding Time
MathFlare Publishing

MathFlare
MATH WORKBOOK
Grade 3-4
Step by Step Guide and Essential Practice with Answers
Addition Subtraction
Multiplication Division
Place Value and Expanded Notations
Fractions and Geometry
MathFlare Publishing

MathFlare
MATH WORKBOOK
Grade 4
Step by Step Guide and Essential Practice with Answers
Addition Subtraction
Multiplication Division
Place Value and Expanded Notations
Fractions and Geometry
MathFlare Publishing

MathFlare
MATH WORKBOOK
Grade 4-5
Step by Step Guide and Essential Practice with Answers
Multiplication Division
Place Value and Expanded Notations
Fractions and Geometry
Unit Conversion
MathFlare Publishing

MathFlare
Grade 5
MATH WORKBOOK
Step by Step Guide and Essential Practice with Answers
Multiplication Division
Place Value and Expanded Notations
Fractions and Geometry
Unit Conversion
MathFlare Publishing

MathFlare
Grade 5-6
MATH WORKBOOK
Step by Step Guide and Essential Practice with Answers
Multiplication Division
Place Value and Expanded Notations
Fractions and Geometry
Units and Statistics
MathFlare Publishing

MathFlare
Grade 6
MATH WORKBOOK
Step by Step Guide and Essential Practice with Answers
Integers and Statistics
Arithmetic and Pre-Algebra
Fractions and Geometry
Ratio and Percentage
MathFlare Publishing

MathFlare
Grade 6-7
MATH WORKBOOK
Step by Step Guide and Essential Practice with Answers
Arithmetic and Pre-Algebra
Ratio, Percent Proportion
Geometry
Statistics
MathFlare Publishing

MathFlare
Grade 7
MATH WORKBOOK
Step by Step Guide and Essential Practice with Answers
Pre-Algebra
Ratio, Percent Proportion
Geometry
Statistics
MathFlare Publishing

MathFlare
Grade 7-8
MATH WORKBOOK
Step by Step Guide and Essential Practice with Answers
Pre-Algebra
Ratio, Percent Proportion
Geometry and Cartesian Plane
Statistics
MathFlare Publishing

MathFlare
Grade 8-9
MATH WORKBOOK
Step by Step Guide and Essential Practice with Answers
Pre-Algebra
Ratio, Proportion and Percentage
Linear Equations
Geometry and Cartesian Plane
MathFlare Publishing

MathFlare
Grade 8
MATH WORKBOOK
Step by Step Guide and Essential Practice with Answers
Pre-Algebra
Percentage
Linear Equations
Geometry
MathFlare Publishing

Chapter. 01

Addition and Subtraction

Addition with Regrouping

When we do addition, we combine numbers. But sometimes, when we're adding numbers, we might need to regroup. Regrouping means we must move a number from one place to another, usually to the next column, to get the right answer.

For Example: Let's take an example of adding 33 and 79 together:

$$33$$
$$+\ \underline{79}$$

First, we start by adding the digits in the ones place: 3 + 9 = 12. We write down the 2 in the ones place and carry over the 1 to the tens place.

$$1$$
$$33$$
$$+\ \underline{79}$$
$$2$$

Now, we add the digits in the tens place, along with the carry-over: 3 + 7 + 1 = 11. We write down the 1 in the tens place and carry over the 1 to the hundreds place.

$$1$$
$$22$$
$$+\ \underline{89}$$
$$111$$

This process of carrying over helps us accurately add numbers, especially when they're larger.

Subtraction with Regrouping

Subtraction is a key math operation where we find the difference between two numbers. Sometimes, when we subtract, we might need to regroup, which means borrowing from the next column.

Let's take an example of subtracting 36 from 63:

First, we start by subtracting the digits in the ones place: 3 - 6. Since 3 is less than 6, we need to regroup. We borrow 1 from the tens place, making it 5 tens instead of 6, and add it to the ones place.

So, 3 becomes 13, and then we subtract 6.

$$
\begin{array}{r}
6\;13 \\
-\;\;3\;\;6 \\
\hline
7
\end{array}
$$

Now, we subtract the tens place digits: 5 - 3 = 2

$$
\begin{array}{r}
5 \\
\cancel{6}\;13 \\
-\;\;3\;\;6 \\
\hline
2\;\;7
\end{array}
$$

This process of regrouping or borrowing helps us accurately subtract numbers, especially when the top digit is smaller than the bottom one.

Let's solve problems from the exercises:

$$
\begin{array}{r}
99 \\
+\;68 \\
\hline
167
\end{array}
\qquad
\begin{array}{r}
33 \\
-\;28 \\
\hline
5
\end{array}
$$

Addition and Subtraction: Unknown Numbers

When we have a situation where we need to find the missing number in an equation, we're usually solving for an unknown.

In this case, we have the equation 20−___=12.

We're trying to figure out what number we need to subtract from 20 to get 12.

We know that 20−___=12, so we can subtract 12 from 20:

$$20 - 12 = 8$$

Let's solve problems from exercises:

$$63 + \underline{\ 37\ } = 100$$

$$25 - \underline{\ 20\ } = 5$$

Word Problems

Word problems are like little puzzles that help us use addition in real-life situations.

For instance:

1. Jake has 6 carrots. He gets 2 more carrots. How many carrots does he have now?

To find out how many carrots he has now, we add the number of carrots he started with (6) to the number of carrots he got (2).

So, we add 6 + 2, which equals 8.

Jake now has 8 carrots in total!

2. Jake saved up 4 dollars to buy pencils. He spent 2 dollars on it. How much money does he have left?

To solve this problem, we need to start with the number of dollars Jake started with and subtract the number of dollars he spent on the pencils.

So, we subtract 2 from 4, which equals 2:

Jake has 2 dollars left after buying the pencils.

We need to understand what the problem is asking and what information it provides. Then, we can use addition or subtraction, depending on whether we're combining or taking away objects, to find the answer.

Let's solve problems from exercises:

Adalyn rode a horse for 7 miles yesterday and 20 miles today. In total, how many miles did she ride?

$$
\begin{array}{r}
7 \quad \text{miles yesterday} \\
+\ 20 \quad \text{miles today} \\
\hline
27 \quad \text{Adalyn rode 27 miles in total}
\end{array}
$$

Emma and Sharon had 5 maps altogether. Sharon gave 3 maps   to Billy. How many maps do they have left?

$$
\begin{array}{r}
5 \quad \text{Emma and Sharon have 5 maps} \\
-\ 3 \quad \text{Sharon Gave 3 maps to Billy} \\
\hline
2 \quad \text{they have 2 maps left}
\end{array}
$$

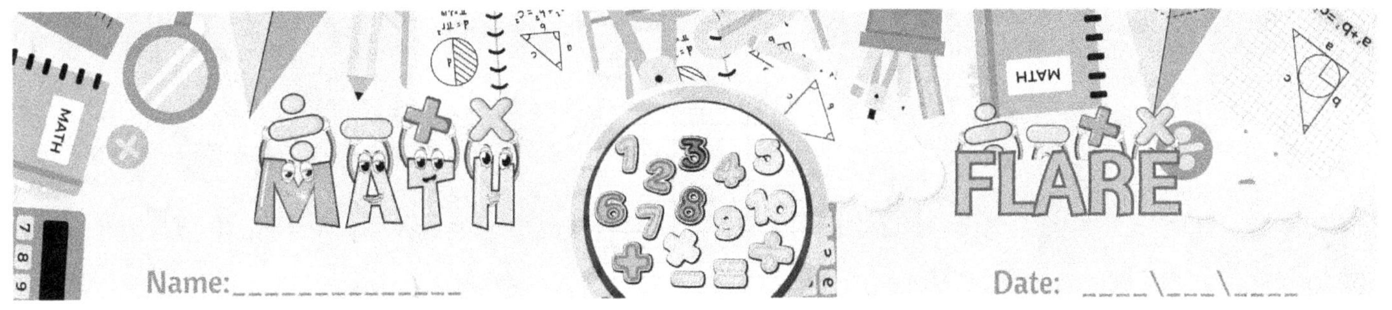

Name:_______________   Date: _______________

Addition: 1 through 100

Find the Sum.

1)   99
   + 68
   ——
    167

2)   73
   + 90
   ——
    163

3)   58
   + 4
   ——

4)   21
   + 46
   ——

5)   15
   + 76
   ——

6)   17
   + 82
   ——

7)   14
   + 33
   ——

8)   4
   + 99
   ——

9)   75
   + 80
   ——

10)   91
    + 39
    ——

11)   7
    + 21
    ——

12)   57
    + 24
    ——

13)   47
    + 82
    ——

14)   33
    + 86
    ——

15)   55
    + 46
    ——

16)   92
    + 21
    ——

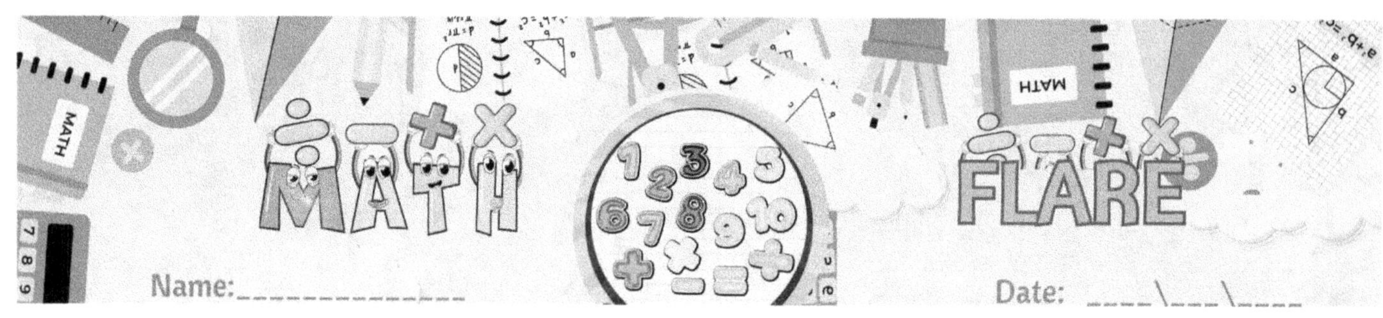

17) 64 + 85	18) 69 + 100	19) 42 + 64	20) 27 + 46
21) 53 + 56	22) 29 + 53	23) 43 + 34	24) 7 + 39
25) 59 + 34	26) 25 + 18	27) 5 + 74	28) 33 + 79
29) 12 + 50	30) 44 + 76	31) 71 + 35	32) 91 + 68
33) 84 + 96	34) 19 + 29	35) 64 + 4	36) 57 + 12

MathFlare - Math Workbook 2nd Grade

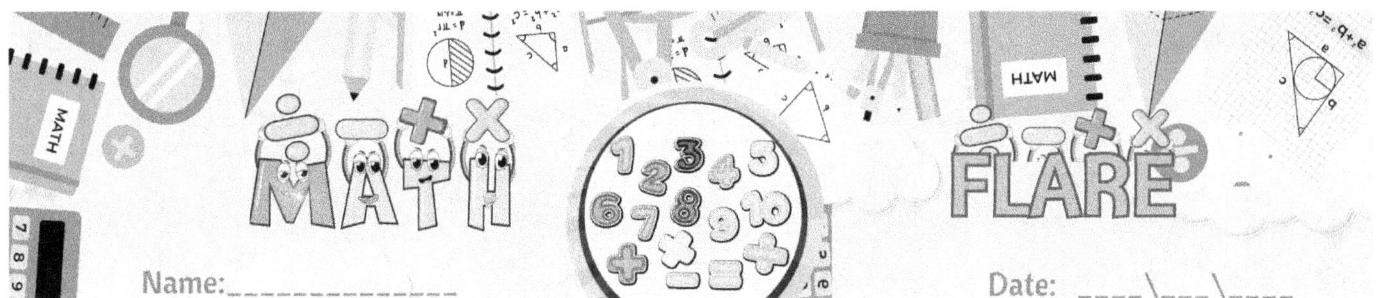

Name:_________________   Date: ______________

37) 54
   + 46
   _____

38) 86
   + 50
   _____

39) 92
   + 5
   _____

40) 81
   + 14
   _____

41) 77
   + 94
   _____

42) 28
   + 22
   _____

43) 22
   + 75
   _____

44) 17
   + 90
   _____

45) 53
   + 89
   _____

46) 89
   + 92
   _____

47) 21
   + 51
   _____

48) 75
   + 19
   _____

49) 65
   + 61
   _____

50) 68
   + 47
   _____

51) 16
   + 78
   _____

52) 75
   + 56
   _____

53) 77
   + 15
   _____

54) 64
   + 59
   _____

55) 88
   + 83
   _____

56) 88
   + 8
   _____

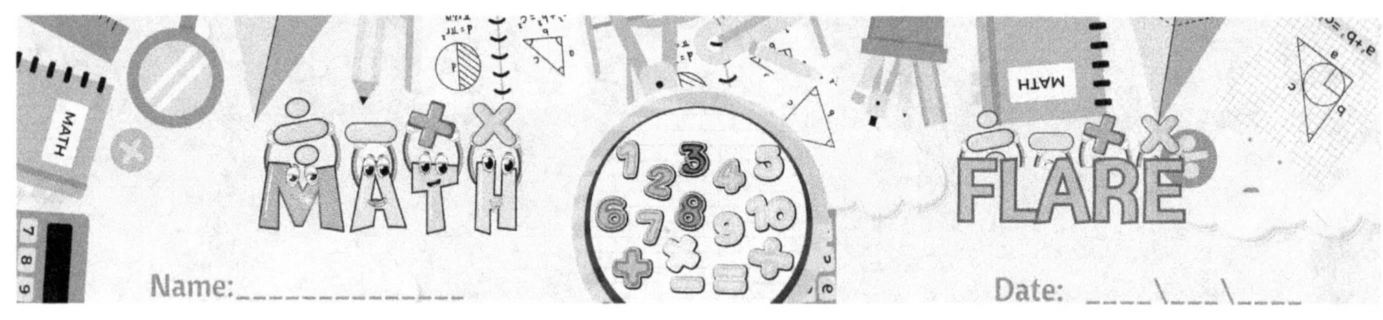

57)	58)	59)	60)
69 + 32	99 + 77	8 + 70	47 + 11

61)	62)	63)	64)
80 + 29	76 + 75	16 + 65	91 + 4

65)	66)	67)	68)
71 + 68	85 + 31	37 + 35	97 + 99

69)	70)	71)	72)
20 + 72	46 + 8	12 + 59	3 + 70

73)	74)	75)	76)
3 + 82	24 + 89	52 + 98	12 + 96

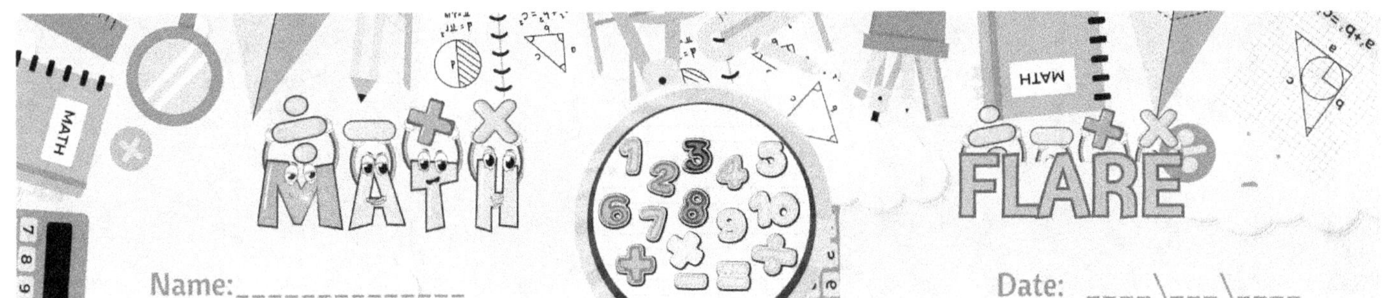

Name:________________   Date: _______________

| 77)   15
+ 59 | 78)   68
+ 87 | 79)   3
+ 100 | 80)   41
+ 12 |

| 81)   24
+ 61 | 82)   88
+ 21 | 83)   98
+ 57 | 84)   34
+   1 |

| 85)   58
+ 37 | 86)   25
+ 40 | 87)   99
+ 22 | 88)   28
+   7 |

| 89)   74
+ 34 | 90)   42
+   3 | 91)   52
+ 73 | 92)   57
+ 89 |

| 93)   18
+ 78 | 94)   67
+ 12 | 95)   97
+ 20 | 96)   31
+ 35 |

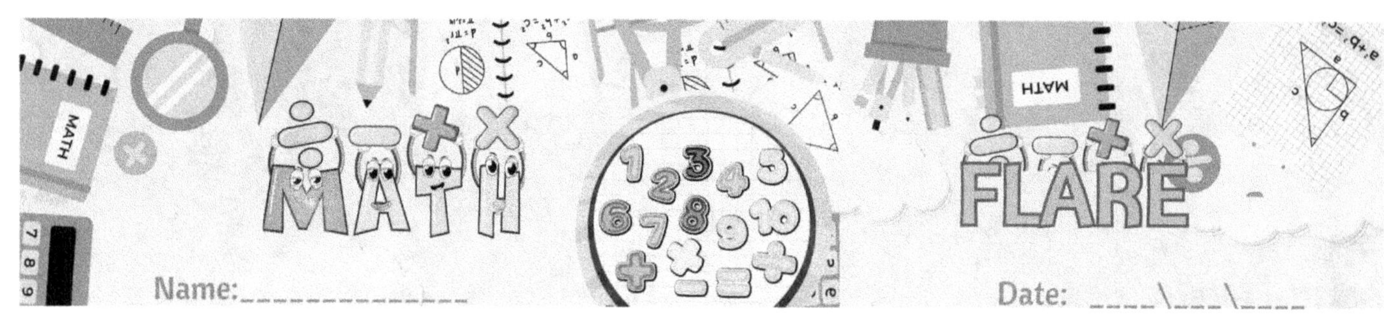

97) 85 + 50	98) 71 + 82	99) 72 + 45	100) 12 + 89
101) 56 + 52	102) 40 + 75	103) 72 + 75	104) 60 + 47
105) 60 + 96	106) 27 + 9	107) 70 + 22	108) 11 + 15
109) 64 + 10	110) 41 + 93	111) 68 + 23	112) 4 + 39
113) 6 + 90	114) 55 + 50	115) 50 + 46	116) 34 + 29

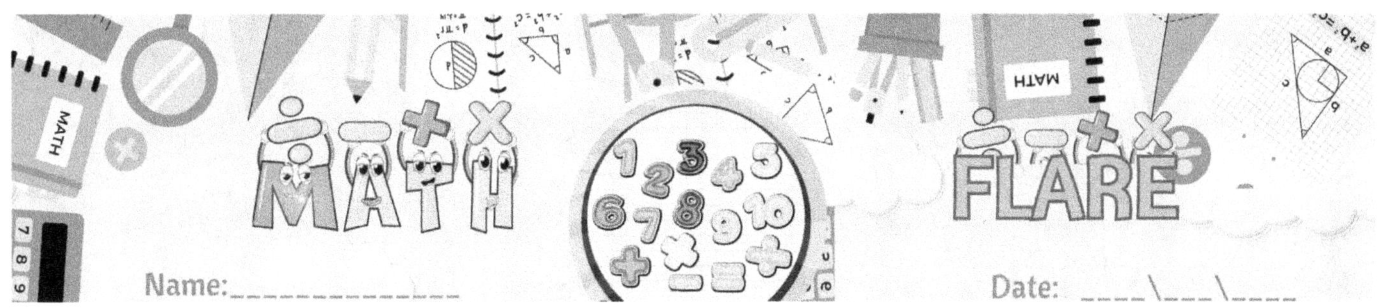

117) 23
    + 53
    _____

118) 47
    + 100
    _____

119) 34
    + 82
    _____

120) 18
    + 43
    _____

121) 19
    + 22
    _____

122) 52
    + 2
    _____

123) 93
    + 24
    _____

124) 64
    + 63
    _____

125) 41
    + 57
    _____

126) 19
    + 64
    _____

127)   5
    + 19
    _____

128) 22
    + 34
    _____

129) 49
    + 2
    _____

130) 70
    + 82
    _____

131) 20
    + 11
    _____

132) 96
    + 15
    _____

133) 63
    + 98
    _____

134) 85
    + 18
    _____

135) 76
    + 11
    _____

136) 81
    + 82
    _____

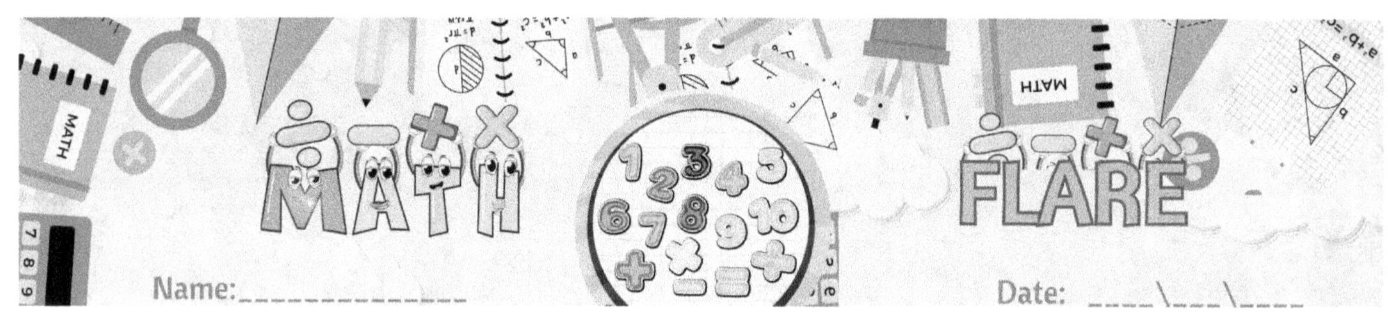

Name:_______________________   Date: _______________

137)   92
      + 98
      ______

138)   75
      + 47
      ______

139)   71
      + 4
      ______

140)   46
      + 83
      ______

141)   27
      + 92
      ______

142)   10
      + 93
      ______

143)   29
      + 71
      ______

144)   25
      + 5
      ______

145)   32
      + 14
      ______

146)   52
      + 33
      ______

147)   13
      + 36
      ______

148)   24
      + 9
      ______

149)   25
      + 38
      ______

150)   39
      + 95
      ______

151)   38
      + 47
      ______

152)   88
      + 31
      ______

153)   76
      + 37
      ______

154)   72
      + 8
      ______

155)   44
      + 75
      ______

156)   62
      + 46
      ______

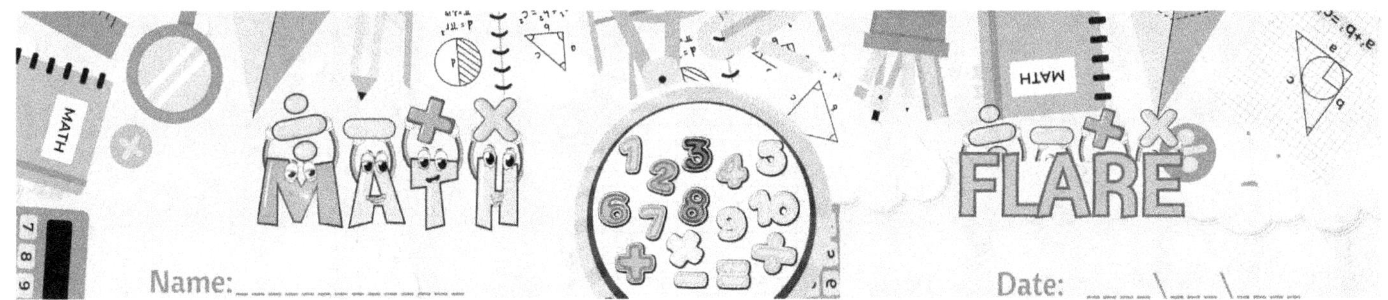

157)   56
     + 87
     ____

158)   57
     + 28
     ____

159)   2
     + 4
     ____

160)   86
     + 92
     ____

161)   74
     + 81
     ____

162)   86
     + 63
     ____

163)   59
     + 50
     ____

164)   70
     + 57
     ____

165)   75
     + 66
     ____

166)   23
     + 34
     ____

167)   65
     + 51
     ____

168)   45
     + 79
     ____

169)   5
     + 79
     ____

170)   19
     + 92
     ____

171)   99
     + 18
     ____

172)   61
     + 57
     ____

173)   52
     + 7
     ____

174)   76
     + 26
     ____

175)   79
     + 95
     ____

176)   8
     + 23
     ____

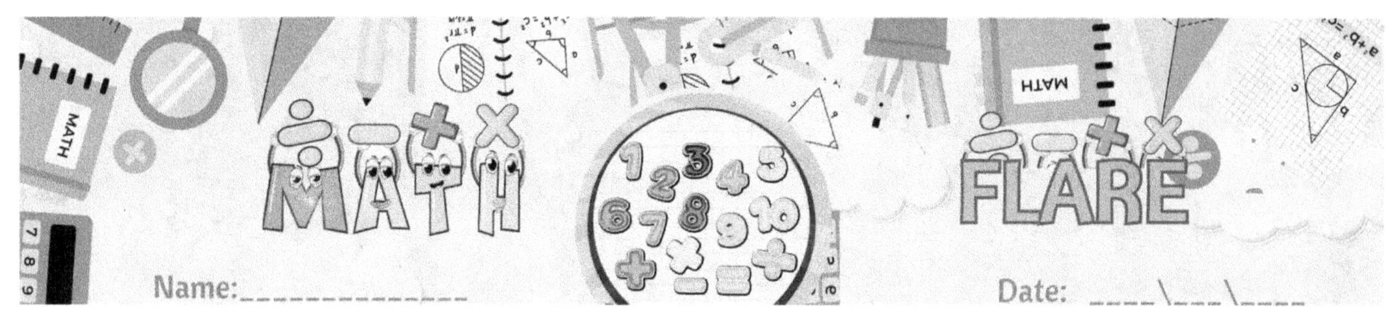

177)	52 + 47	178)	23 + 57	179)	61 + 26	180)	72 + 27
181)	67 + 15	182)	33 + 78	183)	53 + 29	184)	81 + 6
185)	43 + 77	186)	24 + 23	187)	85 + 94	188)	93 + 56
189)	21 + 31	190)	12 + 53	191)	73 + 45	192)	78 + 80
193)	60 + 1	194)	82 + 19	195)	29 + 88	196)	19 + 79

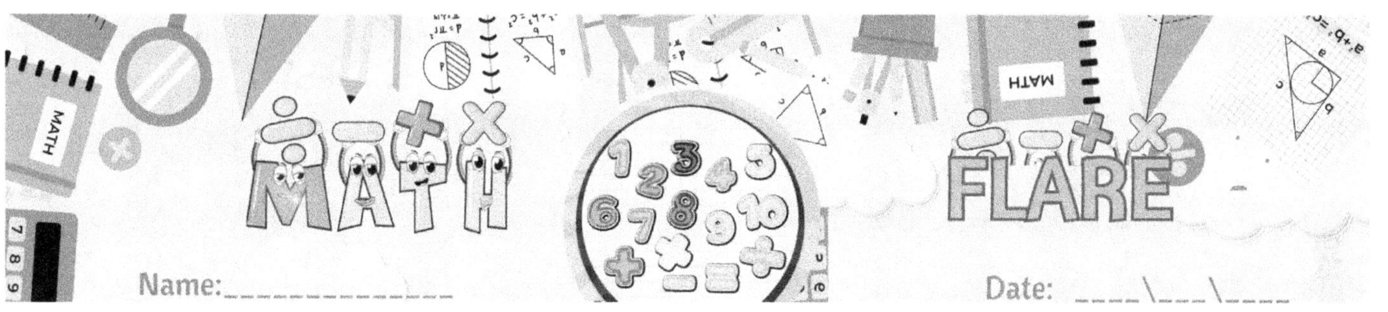

Subtraction: 1 through 100

Find the Difference.

1) 16 − 15 —— 1	2) 33 − 28 —— 5	3) 87 − 73 ——	4) 13 − 4 ——
5) 33 − 24 ——	6) 85 − 3 ——	7) 75 − 63 ——	8) 43 − 25 ——
9) 58 − 39 ——	10) 43 − 14 ——	11) 23 − 5 ——	12) 58 − 14 ——
13) 43 − 23 ——	14) 26 − 14 ——	15) 52 − 33 ——	16) 79 − 43 ——

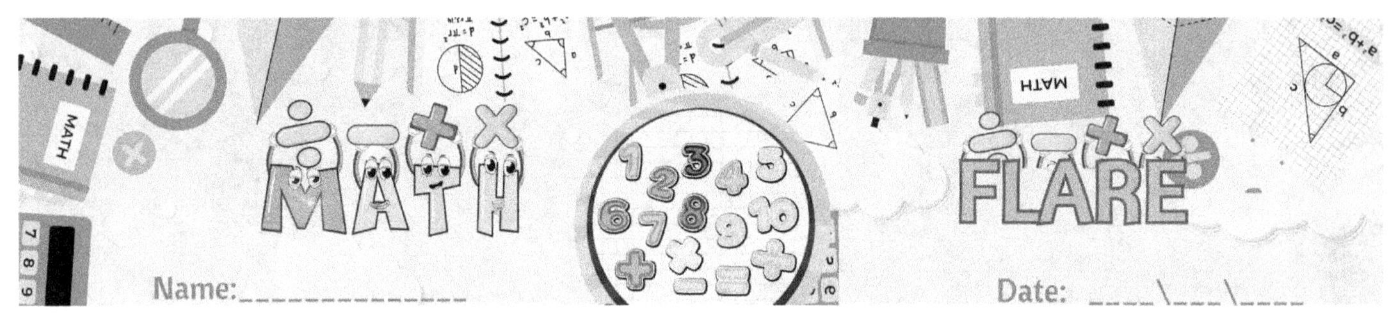

17) 63 − 29	18) 24 − 22	19) 72 − 7	20) 74 − 27
21) 34 − 30	22) 34 − 2	23) 65 − 50	24) 17 − 13
25) 67 − 17	26) 69 − 44	27) 56 − 49	28) 68 − 60
29) 45 − 2	30) 54 − 18	31) 69 − 35	32) 79 − 50
33) 94 − 28	34) 49 − 14	35) 72 − 32	36) 89 − 40

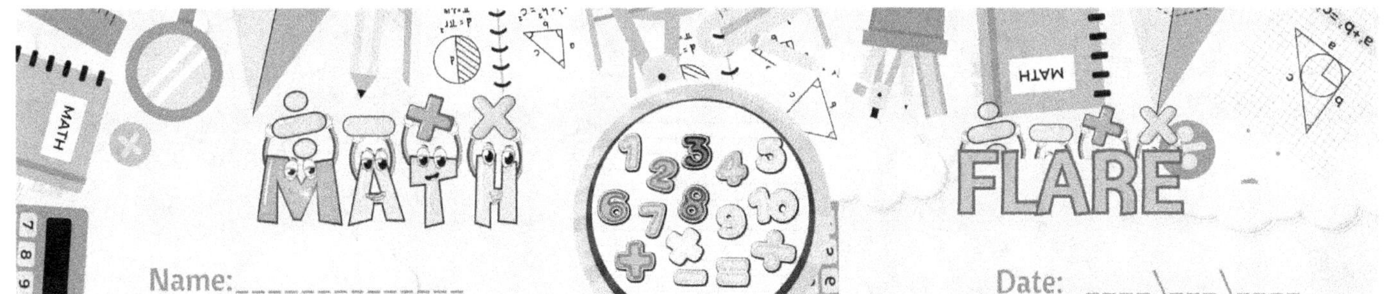

37)   96
  − 2
	38) 14
	  − 5
		39) 93
		  − 48
			40) 66
			  − 40

41)   50
  − 22
	42) 91
	  − 20
		43) 98
		  − 15
			44) 13
			  − 10

45)   83
  − 24
	46) 59
	  − 40
		47) 64
		  − 25
			48) 74
			  − 57

49)   19
  − 13
	50) 17
	  − 6
		51) 40
		  − 33
			52) 16
			  − 4

53)   43
  − 10
	54) 71
	  − 36
		55) 85
		  − 32
			56) 96
			  − 84

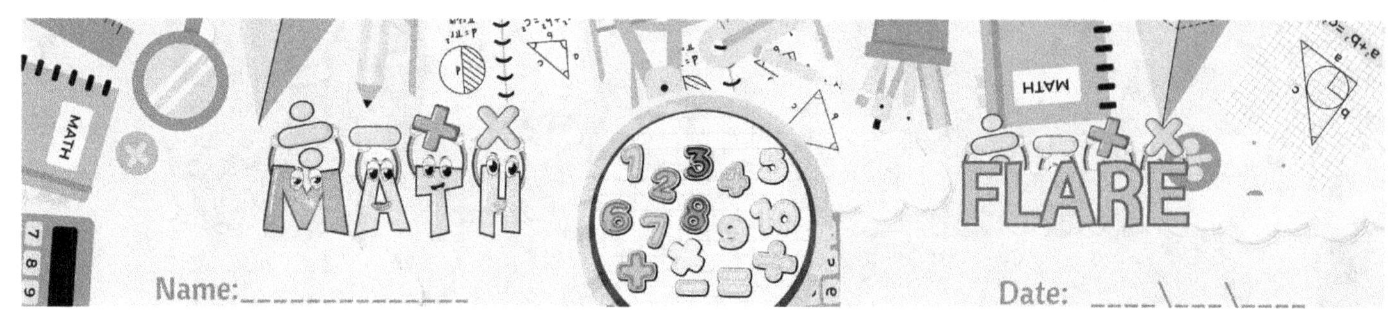

57) 47
  − 42
	58) 89
	  − 21
		59) 64
		  − 36
			60) 69
			  − 55

61) 51
  − 21
	62) 90
	  − 20
		63) 86
		  − 50
			64) 37
			  − 11

65) 25
  − 8
	66) 48
	  − 15
		67) 34
		  − 22
			68) 43
			  − 31

69) 86
  − 67
	70) 52
	  − 28
		71) 40
		  − 27
			72) 55
			  − 27

73) 24
  − 14
	74) 99
	  − 29
		75) 15
		  − 10
			76) 42
			  − 28

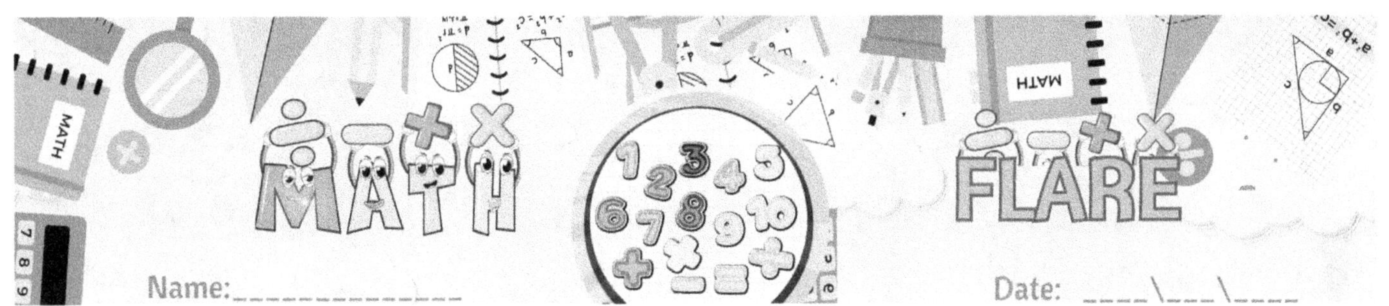

77) 37 − 7	78) 42 − 5	79) 28 − 16	80) 28 − 19
81) 50 − 6	82) 66 − 17	83) 87 − 78	84) 74 − 65
85) 39 − 29	86) 86 − 3	87) 17 − 4	88) 96 − 14
89) 17 − 14	90) 21 − 13	91) 37 − 6	92) 32 − 21
93) 36 − 26	94) 47 − 33	95) 48 − 18	96) 40 − 13

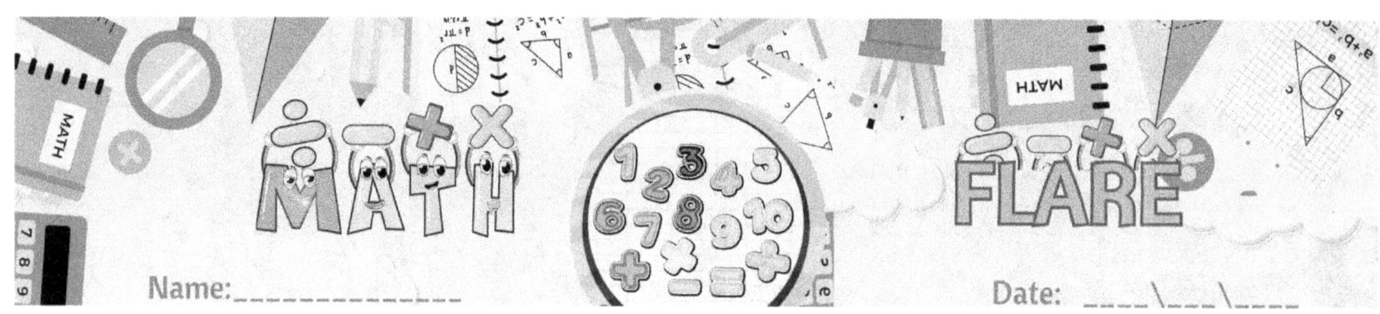

97)	98)	99)	100)
30 − 5	19 − 6	67 − 18	85 − 10

101)	102)	103)	104)
97 − 33	78 − 27	62 − 6	28 − 7

105)	106)	107)	108)
12 − 5	49 − 29	44 − 14	88 − 84

109)	110)	111)	112)
54 − 2	52 − 50	45 − 25	80 − 34

113)	114)	115)	116)
99 − 80	14 − 12	27 − 23	81 − 16

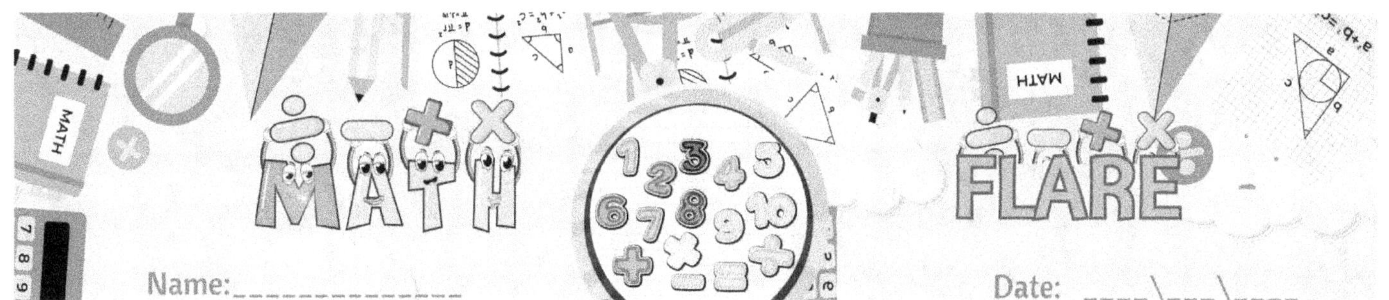

Name: _______________   Date: ____________

117) 26
    - 24
    ______

118) 91
    - 87
    ______

119) 22
    - 8
    ______

120) 53
    - 11
    ______

121) 41
    - 39
    ______

122) 89
    - 59
    ______

123) 36
    - 33
    ______

124) 35
    - 6
    ______

125) 38
    - 19
    ______

126) 79
    - 64
    ______

127) 68
    - 2
    ______

128) 94
    - 22
    ______

129) 60
    - 10
    ______

130) 18
    - 8
    ______

131) 26
    - 6
    ______

132) 26
    - 15
    ______

133) 22
    - 21
    ______

134) 15
    - 15
    ______

135) 10
    - 2
    ______

136) 59
    - 16
    ______

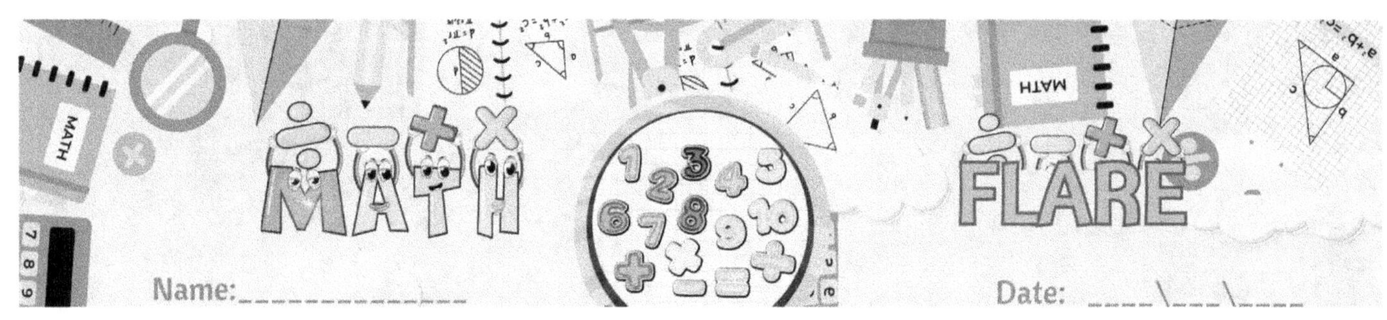

137) 64 − 28	138) 69 − 9	139) 22 − 3	140) 57 − 52
141) 56 − 40	142) 18 − 18	143) 58 − 10	144) 98 − 67
145) 46 − 45	146) 31 − 3	147) 12 − 3	148) 80 − 24
149) 89 − 10	150) 81 − 27	151) 54 − 33	152) 34 − 14
153) 47 − 24	154) 61 − 27	155) 13 − 1	156) 89 − 25

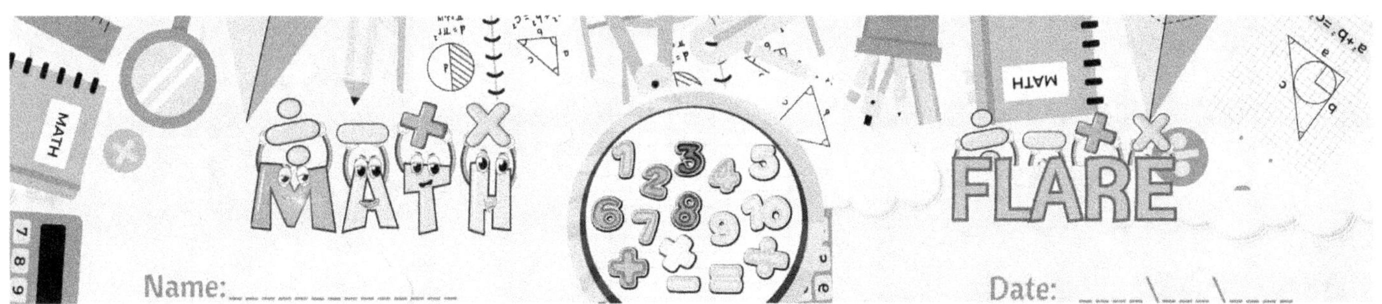

Name: _______________________   Date: _______________

| 157) 72
  - 35 | 158) 54
  - 43 | 159) 68
  - 66 | 160) 98
  - 38 |

| 161) 63
  - 3 | 162) 94
  - 44 | 163) 32
  - 15 | 164) 69
  - 26 |

| 165) 31
  - 2 | 166) 36
  - 8 | 167) 84
  - 17 | 168) 30
  - 15 |

| 169) 75
  - 12 | 170) 78
  - 37 | 171) 20
  - 19 | 172) 95
  - 21 |

| 173) 28
  - 21 | 174) 51
  - 16 | 175) 82
  - 7 | 176) 50
  - 41 |

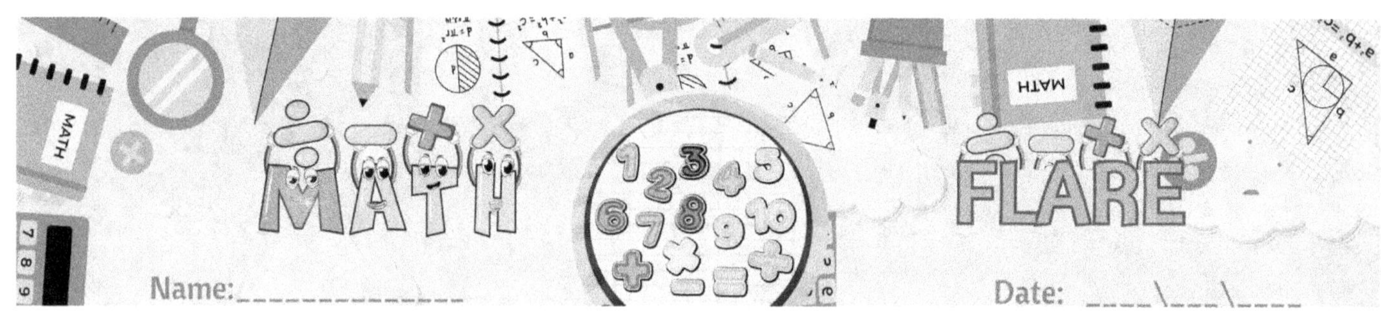

177)   42
  − 30

178)   75
  − 35

179)   70
  − 56

180)   23
  − 22

181)   87
  − 18

182)   28
  − 28

183)   76
  − 53

184)   51
  − 26

185)   33
  − 1

186)   17
  − 9

187)   29
  − 15

188)   33
  − 17

189)   10
  − 4

190)   63
  − 30

191)   85
  − 11

192)   53
  − 41

193)   83
  − 77

194)   11
  − 9

195)   66
  − 60

196)   78
  − 74

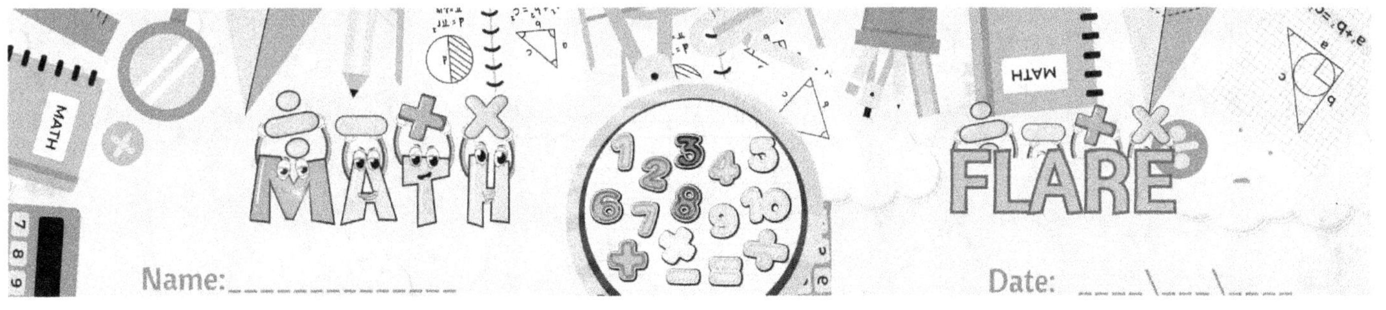

Addition with Regrouping

Find the sum.

1)
```
   48
 + 83
 ----
  131
```

2)
```
   31
 + 99
 ----
  130
```

3)
```
    5
 + 85
 ----
```

4)
```
    1
 + 99
 ----
```

5)
```
   62
 + 88
 ----
```

6)
```
   44
 + 78
 ----
```

7)
```
   38
 + 95
 ----
```

8)
```
   55
 + 66
 ----
```

9)
```
   95
 + 57
 ----
```

10)
```
   65
 +  5
 ----
```

11)
```
   42
 + 78
 ----
```

12)
```
   86
 + 34
 ----
```

13)
```
    3
 + 57
 ----
```

14)
```
   21
 + 89
 ----
```

15)
```
   49
 + 81
 ----
```

16)
```
   89
 + 36
 ----
```

17)
```
   87
 + 84
 ----
```

18)
```
   25
 + 85
 ----
```

19)
```
   21
 +  9
 ----
```

20)
```
   32
 + 78
 ----
```

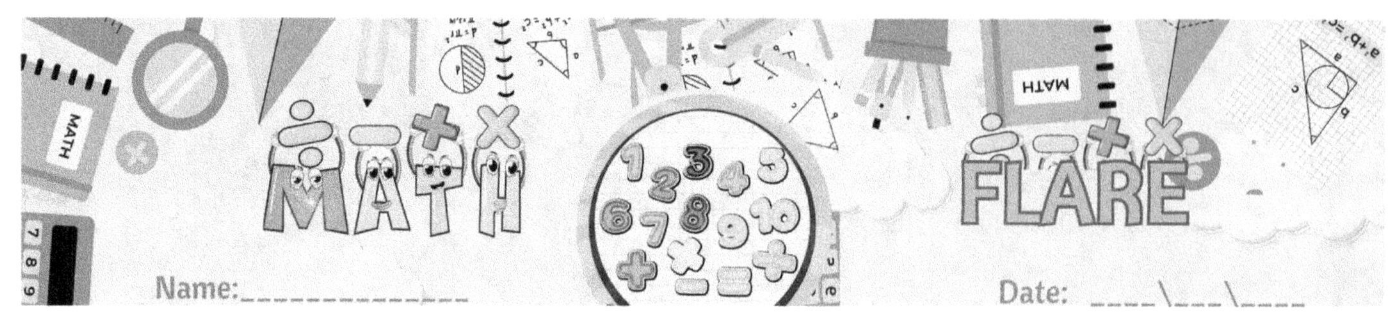

21) 16 + 96	22) 85 + 99	23) 69 + 89	24) 39 + 87
25) 39 + 76	26) 85 + 57	27) 27 + 96	28) 55 + 58
29) 66 + 96	30) 94 + 59	31) 61 + 89	32) 47 + 77
33) 96 + 9	34) 23 + 88	35) 71 + 79	36) 46 + 98
37) 89 + 78	38) 42 + 88	39) 65 + 67	40) 12 + 99

41)   77
     + 34
     ______

42)   56
     + 77
     ______

43)   11
     + 99
     ______

44)   59
     + 4
     ______

45)   17
     + 95
     ______

46)   3
     + 67
     ______

47)   16
     + 99
     ______

48)   91
     + 99
     ______

49)   93
     + 38
     ______

50)   83
     + 79
     ______

51)   79
     + 79
     ______

52)   32
     + 79
     ______

53)   44
     + 89
     ______

54)   66
     + 76
     ______

55)   98
     + 8
     ______

56)   67
     + 68
     ______

57)   69
     + 72
     ______

58)   82
     + 49
     ______

59)   74
     + 59
     ______

60)   62
     + 79
     ______

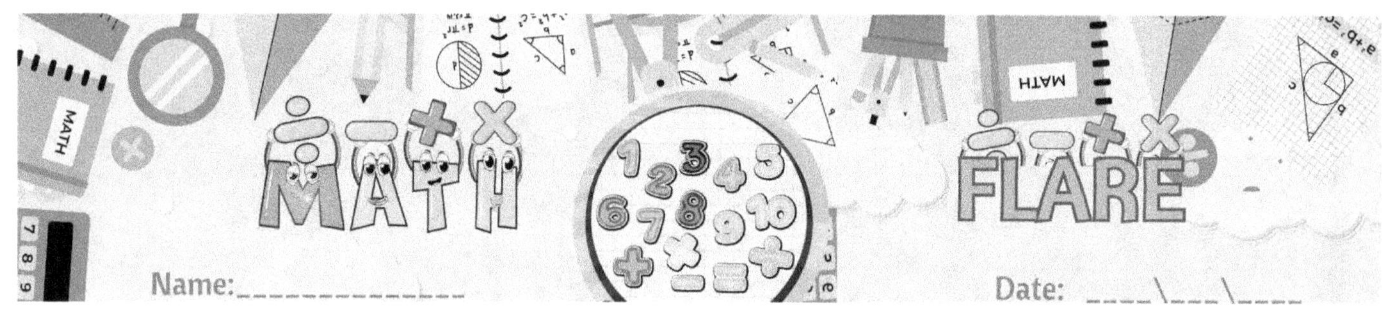

61) 84 + 9	62) 48 + 98	63) 18 + 98	64) 24 + 96
65) 84 + 78	66) 33 + 88	67) 93 + 79	68) 34 + 87
69) 22 + 88	70) 99 + 83	71) 63 + 87	72) 48 + 78
73) 91 + 69	74) 13 + 97	75) 64 + 58	76) 16 + 6
77) 95 + 27	78) 83 + 47	79) 11 + 9	80) 37 + 97

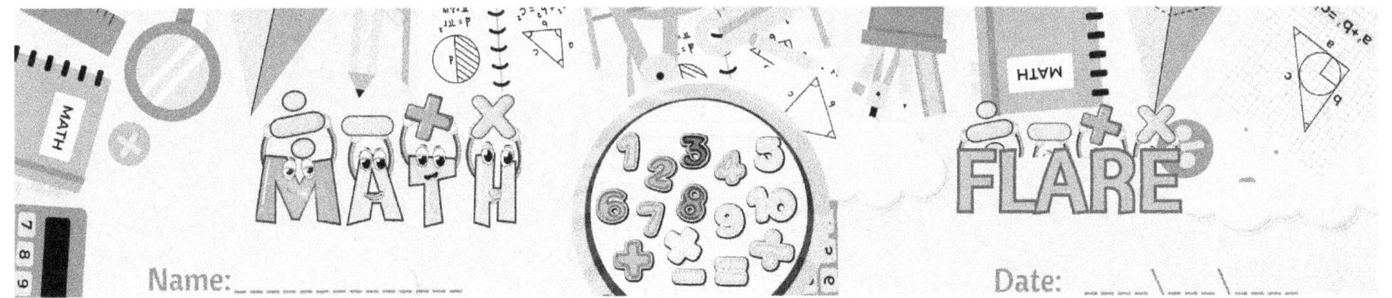

81) 75 + 89	82) 29 + 4	83) 9 + 86	84) 38 + 78
85) 78 + 3	86) 42 + 98	87) 51 + 69	88) 27 + 85
89) 49 + 94	90) 9 + 9	91) 68 + 63	92) 97 + 88
93) 77 + 37	94) 74 + 97	95) 35 + 95	96) 5 + 56
97) 41 + 79	98) 43 + 78	99) 88 + 37	100) 25 + 96

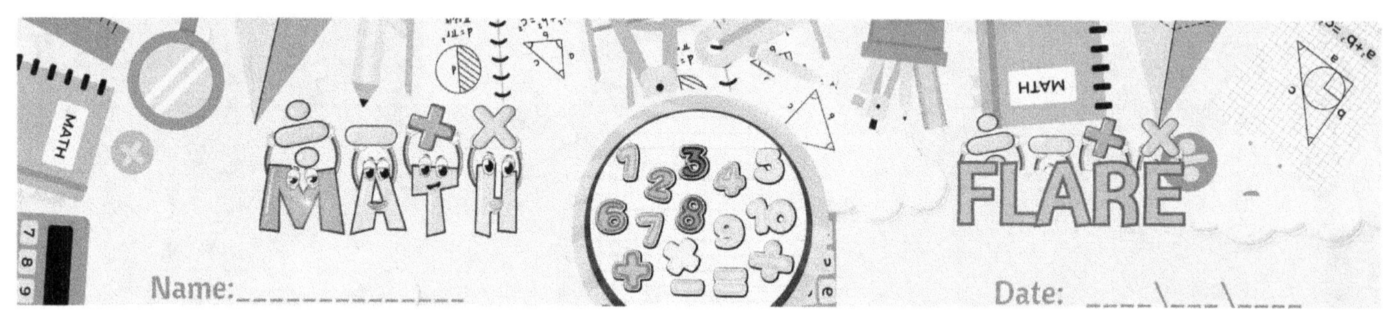

101) 85 + 46	102) 95 + 47	103) 65 + 55	104) 56 + 4
105) 19 + 97	106) 17 + 98	107) 2 + 69	108) 7 + 23
109) 5 + 86	110) 56 + 7	111) 6 + 87	112) 65 + 75
113) 15 + 95	114) 91 + 39	115) 21 + 99	116) 98 + 44
117) 82 + 59	118) 93 + 39	119) 66 + 79	120) 41 + 69

MathFlare - Math Workbook 2nd Grade

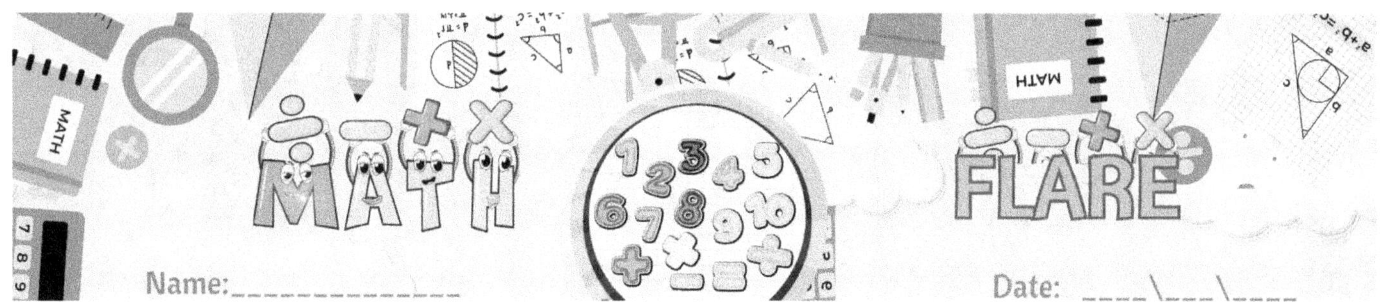

121)   47
     + 83
     ______

122)   52
     + 89
     ______

123)   5
     + 29
     ______

124)   68
     + 86
     ______

125)   33
     + 99
     ______

126)   39
     + 79
     ______

127)   39
     + 9
     ______

128)   77
     + 95
     ______

129)   13
     + 99
     ______

130)   47
     + 85
     ______

131)   24
     + 98
     ______

132)   79
     + 53
     ______

133)   28
     + 96
     ______

134)   45
     + 79
     ______

135)   88
     + 38
     ______

136)   41
     + 89
     ______

137)   23
     + 99
     ______

138)   36
     + 76
     ______

139)   62
     + 48
     ______

140)   99
     + 58
     ______

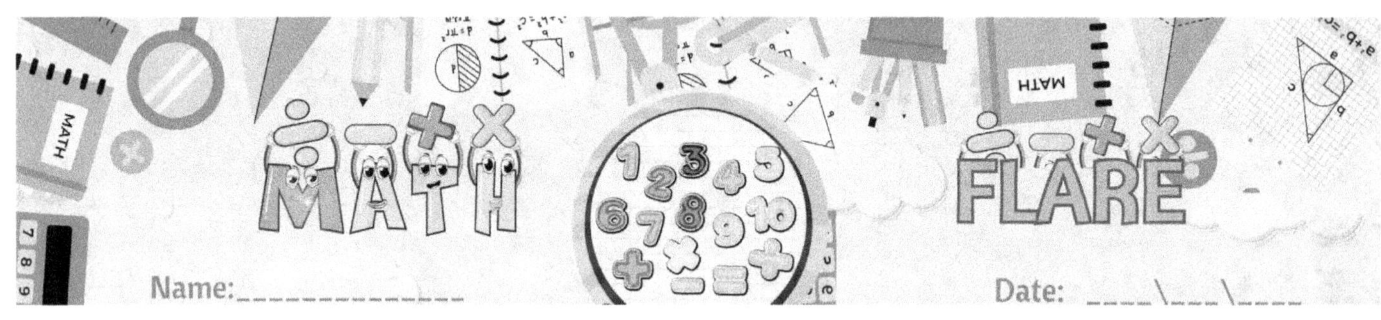

141)   7
 + 4

142)   58
 + 75

143)   79
 + 93

144)   22
 + 99

145)   61
 + 99

146)   1
 + 59

147)   95
 + 95

148)   96
 + 27

149)   91
 + 9

150)   68
 + 95

151)   69
 + 7

152)   81
 + 49

153)   27
 + 8

154)   87
 + 66

155)   53
 + 77

156)   39
 + 93

157)   19
 + 98

158)   81
 + 59

159)   17
 + 99

160)   24
 + 89

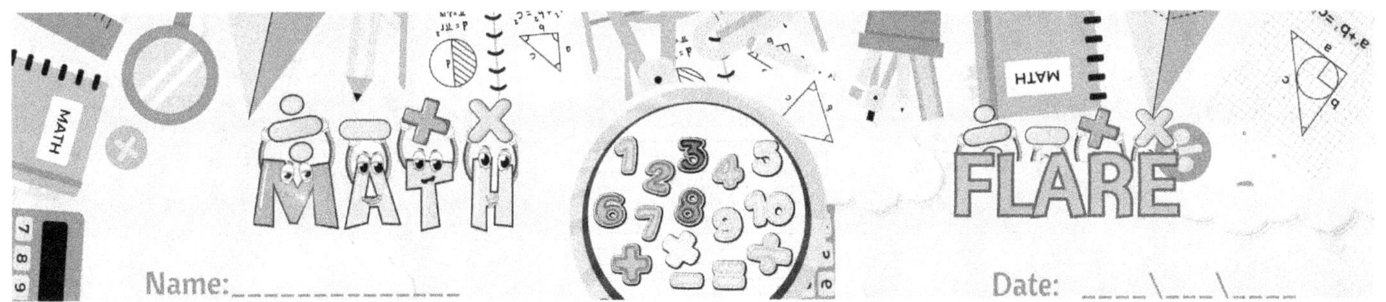

161) 35 + 85	162) 75 + 77	163) 2 + 59	164) 62 + 89
165) 13 + 98	166) 18 + 94	167) 7 + 73	168) 43 + 89
169) 4 + 17	170) 75 + 95	171) 42 + 79	172) 14 + 98
173) 75 + 79	174) 47 + 63	175) 85 + 89	176) 72 + 48
177) 71 + 99	178) 68 + 57	179) 7 + 37	180) 4 + 78

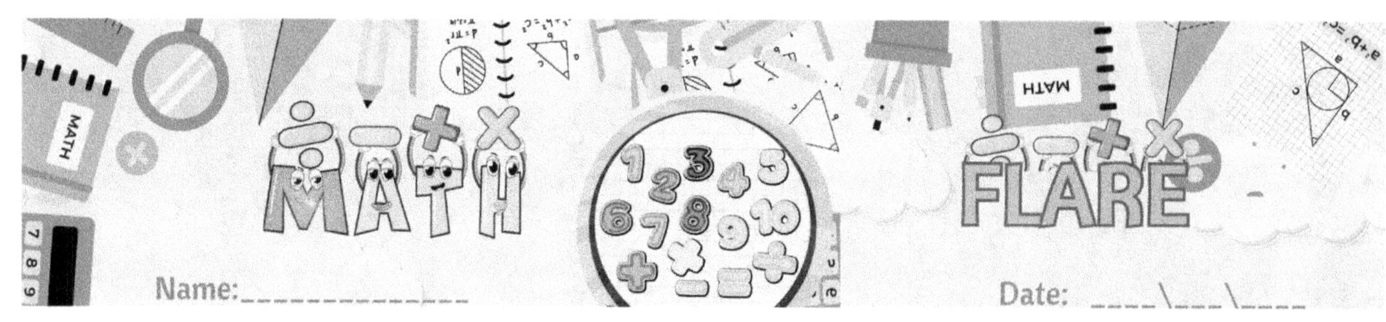

181) 64 + 96	182) 25 + 95	183) 62 + 59	184) 81 + 99
185) 56 + 9	186) 5 + 35	187) 87 + 97	188) 95 + 39
189) 29 + 99	190) 92 + 68	191) 3 + 48	192) 29 + 91
193) 94 + 57	194) 76 + 84	195) 85 + 49	196) 54 + 67
197) 25 + 97	198) 28 + 86	199) 97 + 96	200) 63 + 98

Subtraction with Regrouping

Find the difference.

1) 30
  − 11
  ___
  19

2) 70
  − 8
  ___
  62

3) 90
  − 59
  ___

4) 40
  − 8
  ___

5) 50
  − 42
  ___

6) 90
  − 67
  ___

7) 20
  − 1
  ___

8) 90
  − 71
  ___

9)   5
  − 2
  ___

10) 40
  − 9
  ___

11) 70
  − 59
  ___

12) 30
  − 4
  ___

13) 70
  − 21
  ___

14) 70
  − 63
  ___

15) 30
  − 18
  ___

16) 10
  − 6
  ___

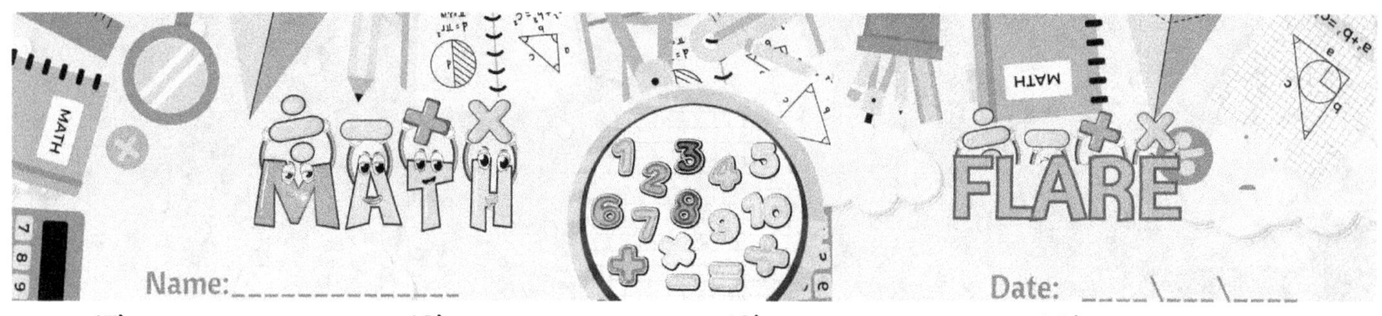

17) 80 − 53	18) 90 − 18	19) 3 − 2	20) 80 − 46
21) 20 − 5	22) 60 − 48	23) 50 − 27	24) 10 − 2
25) 90 − 24	26) 60 − 33	27) 60 − 53	28) 70 − 66
29) 60 − 11	30) 6 − 2	31) 30 − 12	32) 50 − 13
33) 40 − 31	34) 30 − 25	35) 20 − 15	36) 80 − 43

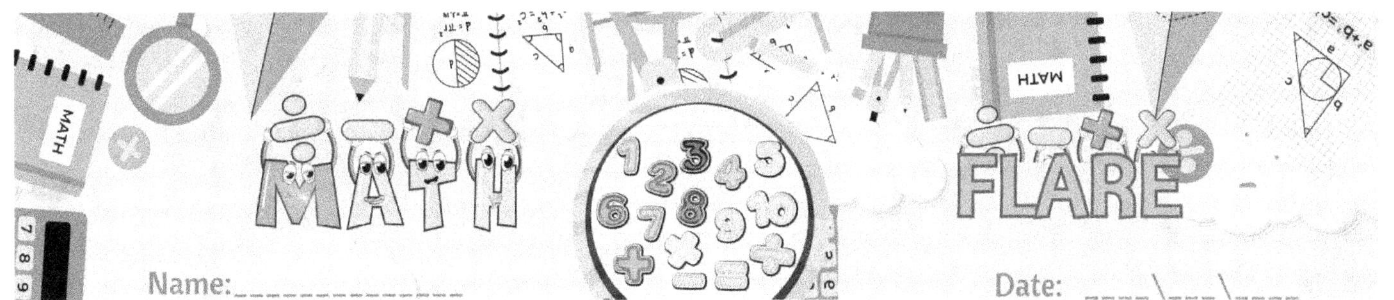

37) 60 − 23	38) 70 − 32	39) 30 − 27	40) 40 − 35
41) 40 − 13	42) 40 − 14	43) 40 − 36	44) 70 − 37
45) 5 − 1	46) 20 − 13	47) 7 − 4	48) 30 − 23
49) 30 − 26	50) 60 − 8	51) 20 − 16	52) 70 − 53
53) 20 − 12	54) 10 − 4	55) 90 − 33	56) 30 − 9

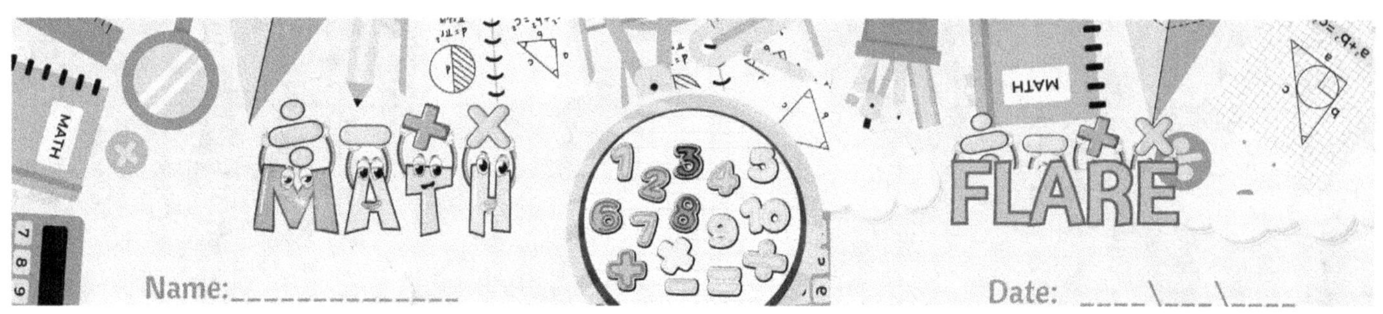

57) 20 − 17	58) 60 − 4	59) 50 − 19	60) 50 − 47
61) 20 − 8	62) 10 − 5	63) 80 − 6	64) 90 − 69
65) 70 − 1	66) 50 − 22	67) 70 − 49	68) 50 − 38
69) 40 − 2	70) 60 − 52	71) 40 − 7	72) 30 − 16
73) 90 − 63	74) 90 − 79	75) 70 − 43	76) 80 − 5

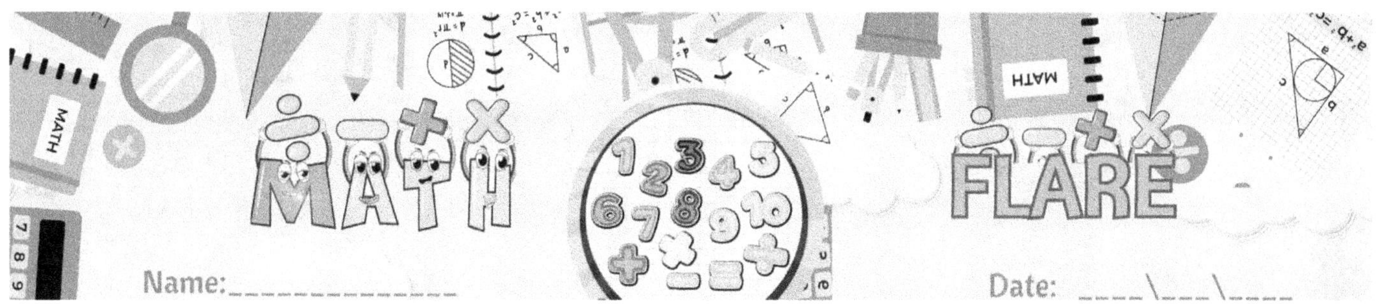

77) 40 − 23	78) 20 − 6	79) 40 − 5	80) 60 − 34
81) 80 − 19	82) 50 − 39	83) 20 − 14	84) 9 − 2
85) 80 − 13	86) 30 − 21	87) 70 − 3	88) 30 − 17
89) 50 − 2	90) 70 − 18	91) 70 − 56	92) 60 − 6
93) 60 − 31	94) 70 − 2	95) 20 − 7	96) 70 − 64

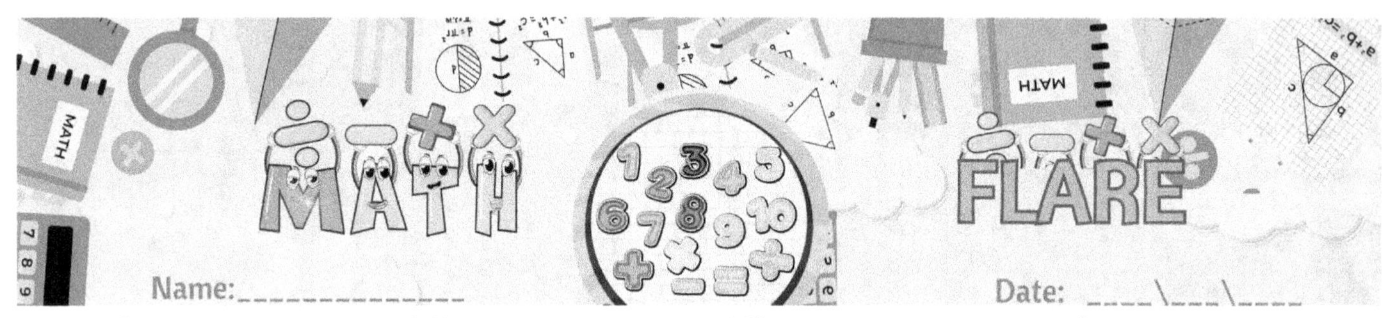

97) 90 − 8	98) 80 − 42	99) 40 − 15	100) 90 − 52
101) 50 − 37	102) 50 − 43	103) 60 − 45	104) 50 − 18
105) 70 − 26	106) 2 − 1	107) 30 − 8	108) 70 − 54
109) 90 − 32	110) 40 − 29	111) 50 − 4	112) 70 − 15
113) 10 − 1	114) 40 − 33	115) 90 − 87	116) 40 − 6

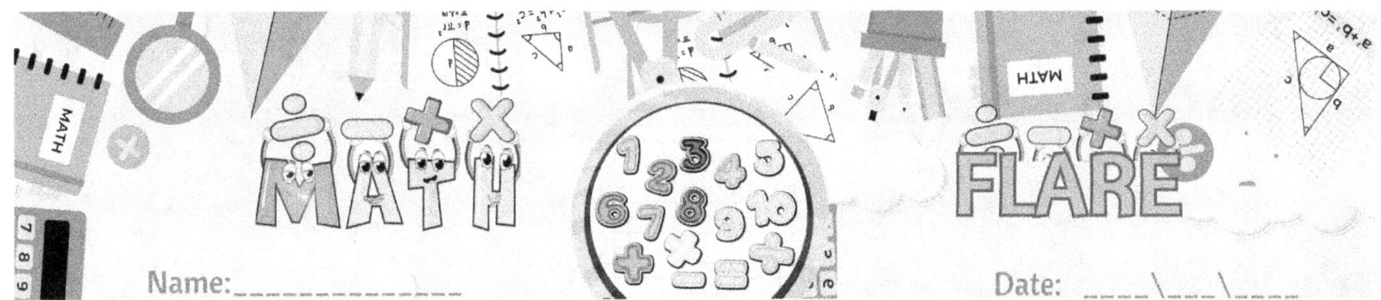

117)   80
  - 3

118)   50
  - 5

119)   80
  - 69

120)   80
  - 2

121)   70
  - 31

122)   90
  - 11

123)   50
  - 17

124)   90
  - 41

125)   70
  - 23

126)   50
  - 23

127)   90
  - 5

128)   70
  - 44

129)   60
  - 25

130)   30
  - 13

131)   80
  - 47

132)   40
  - 4

133)   70
  - 57

134)   90
  - 86

135)   40
  - 21

136)   60
  - 7

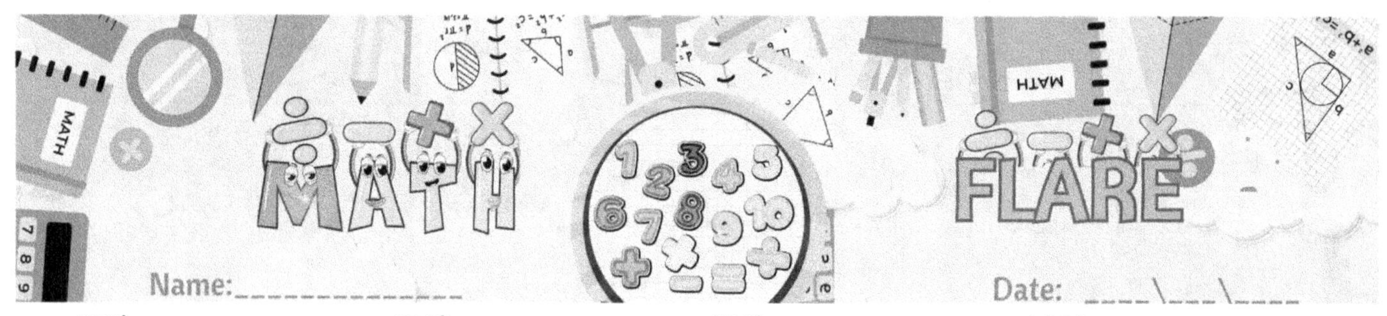

137) 50 - 32	138) 60 - 3	139) 30 - 24	140) 90 - 42
141) 20 - 11	142) 1 - 1	143) 30 - 14	144) 50 - 29
145) 2 - 2	146) 20 - 4	147) 90 - 6	148) 6 - 1
149) 80 - 64	150) 50 - 41	151) 50 - 36	152) 30 - 15
153) 40 - 11	154) 50 - 26	155) 70 - 19	156) 70 - 51

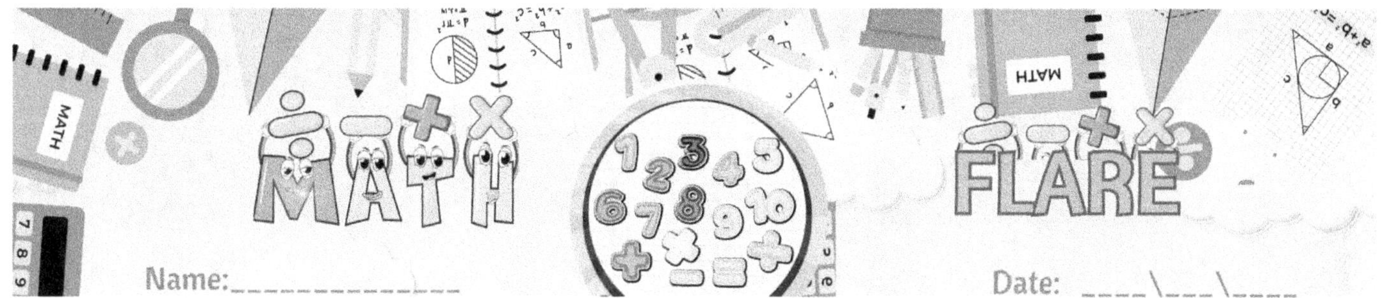

157)   90
    - 22
	158) 60
	    - 26
		159) 90
		    - 53
			160) 50
			    - 24

161)   20
    - 3
	162) 70
	    - 33
		163) 10
		    - 3
			164) 90
			    - 21

165)   80
    - 75
	166) 8
	    - 1
		167) 70
		    - 48
			168) 90
			    - 45

169)   60
    - 22
	170) 70
	    - 39
		171) 10
		    - 7
			172) 80
			    - 36

173)   90
    - 54
	174) 40
	    - 22
		175) 40
		    - 32
			176) 40
			    - 27

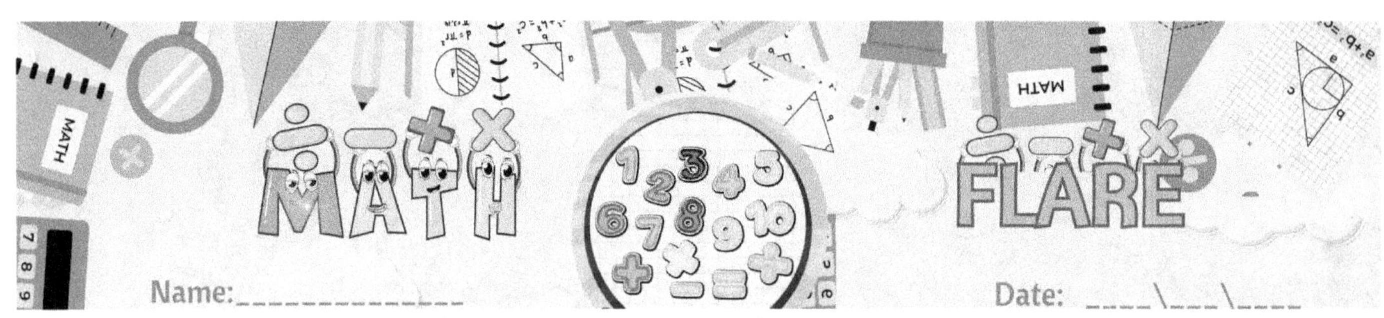

177) 60
    - 14
    ____

178) 70
    - 58
    ____

179) 40
    - 34
    ____

180) 70
    - 22
    ____

181) 70
    - 34
    ____

182) 40
    - 18
    ____

183) 50
    - 33
    ____

184) 60
    - 55
    ____

185) 50
    - 8
    ____

186) 90
    - 12
    ____

187)   9
    - 4
    ____

188) 50
    - 3
    ____

189) 50
    - 44
    ____

190) 30
    - 6
    ____

191) 60
    - 57
    ____

192) 40
    - 37
    ____

193) 90
    - 13
    ____

194) 20
    - 2
    ____

195) 70
    - 67
    ____

196) 50
    - 9
    ____

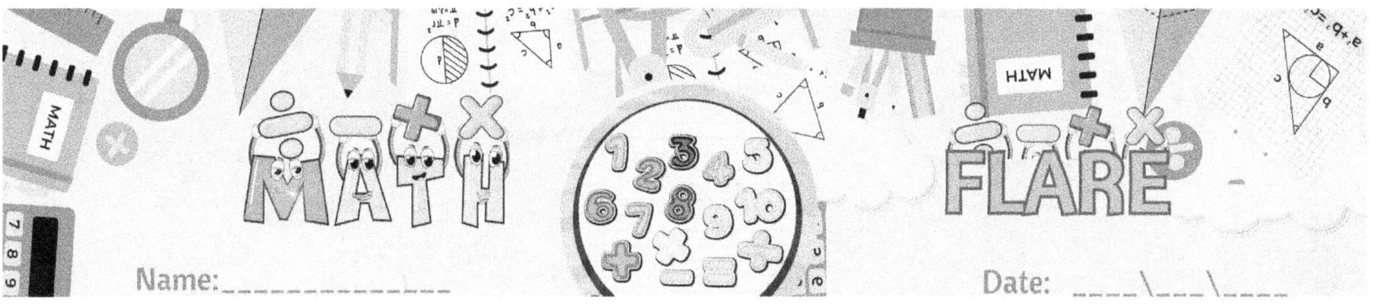

Make 100

Add a number to the first number to make 100.

1) 93 + _7_ = 100

2) 36 + ___ = 100

3) 97 + ___ = 100

4) 86 + ___ = 100

5) 98 + ___ = 100

6) 34 + ___ = 100

7) 1 + ___ = 100

8) 66 + ___ = 100

9) 15 + ___ = 100

10) 31 + ___ = 100

11) 4 + ___ = 100

12) 90 + ___ = 100

13) 22 + ___ = 100

14) 13 + ___ = 100

15) 18 + ___ = 100

16) 69 + ___ = 100

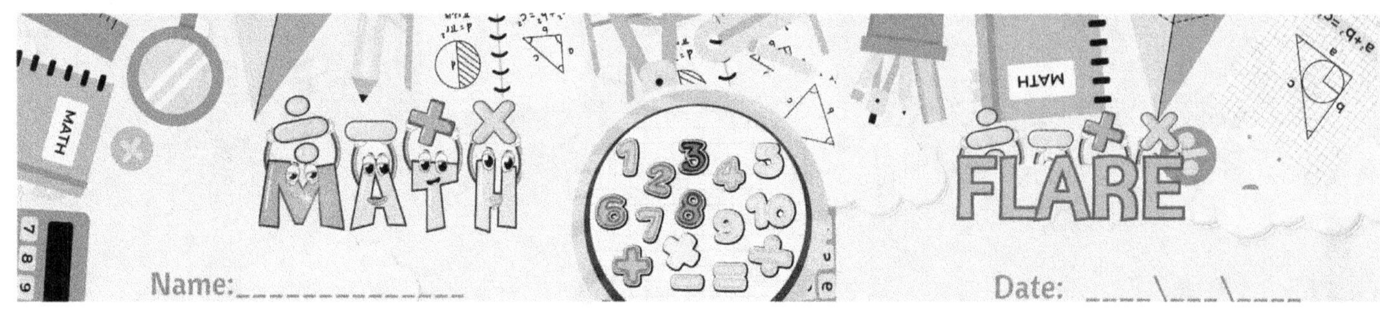

17) 7 + ___ = 100

18) 29 + ___ = 100

19) 57 + ___ = 100

20) 79 + ___ = 100

21) 5 + ___ = 100

22) 21 + ___ = 100

23) 8 + ___ = 100

24) 40 + ___ = 100

25) 82 + ___ = 100

26) 17 + ___ = 100

27) 3 + ___ = 100

28) 72 + ___ = 100

29) 37 + ___ = 100

30) 26 + ___ = 100

31) 83 + ___ = 100

32) 63 + ___ = 100

33) 33 + ___ = 100

34) 27 + ___ = 100

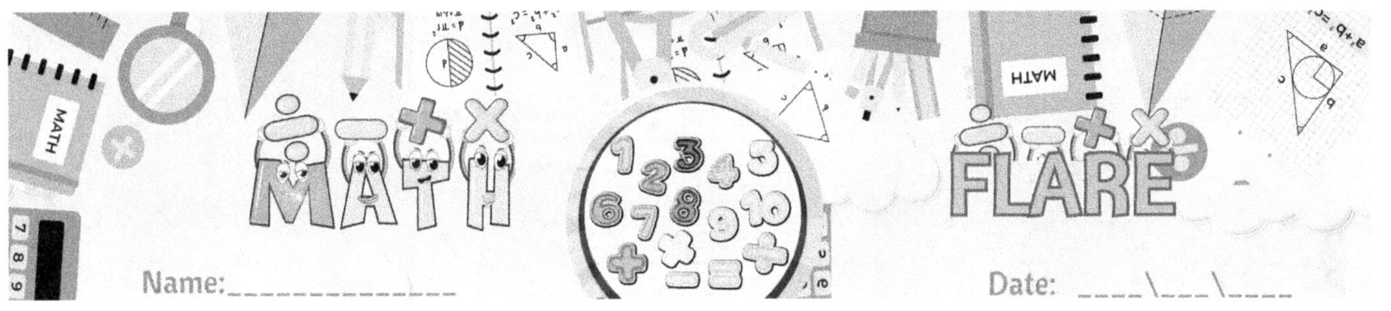

35) 68 + ___ = 100

36) 77 + ___ = 100

37) 94 + ___ = 100

38) 41 + ___ = 100

39) 65 + ___ = 100

40) 52 + ___ = 100

41) 80 + ___ = 100

42) 73 + ___ = 100

43) 95 + ___ = 100

44) 62 + ___ = 100

45) 96 + ___ = 100

46) 88 + ___ = 100

47) 39 + ___ = 100

48) 6 + ___ = 100

49) 19 + ___ = 100

50) 81 + ___ = 100

51) 25 + ___ = 100

52) 47 + ___ = 100

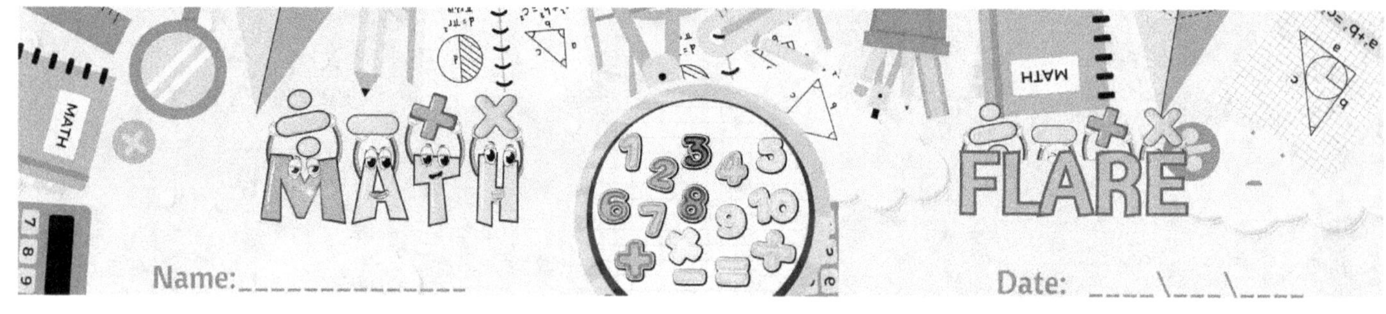

53) 55 + ___ = 100

54) 20 + ___ = 100

55) 46 + ___ = 100

56) 14 + ___ = 100

57) 43 + ___ = 100

58) 51 + ___ = 100

59) 75 + ___ = 100

60) 12 + ___ = 100

61) 53 + ___ = 100

62) 11 + ___ = 100

63) 61 + ___ = 100

64) 76 + ___ = 100

65) 44 + ___ = 100

66) 92 + ___ = 100

67) 32 + ___ = 100

68) 24 + ___ = 100

69) 84 + ___ = 100

70) 30 + ___ = 100

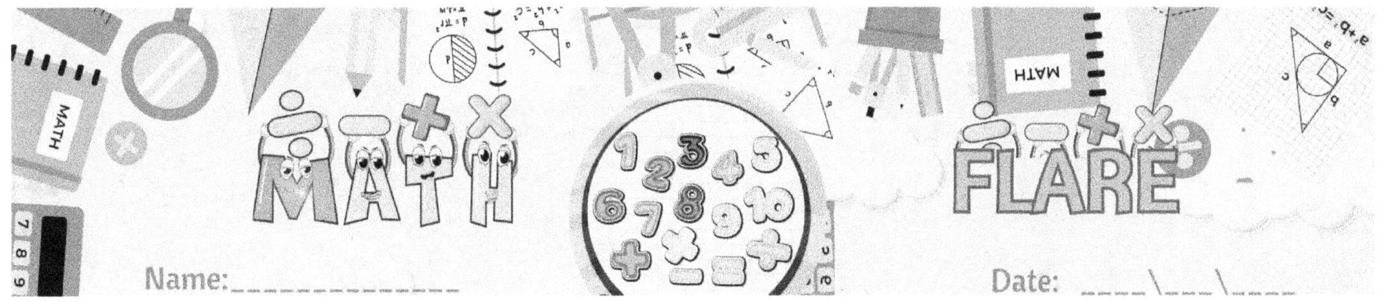

Name:_________________   Date: ____________

71) 78 + ___ = 100

72) 71 + ___ = 100

73) 67 + ___ = 100

74) 16 + ___ = 100

75) 50 + ___ = 100

76) 64 + ___ = 100

77) 48 + ___ = 100

78) 89 + ___ = 100

79) 58 + ___ = 100

80) 85 + ___ = 100

81) 23 + ___ = 100

82) 59 + ___ = 100

83) 10 + ___ = 100

84) 74 + ___ = 100

85) 28 + ___ = 100

86) 87 + ___ = 100

87) 54 + ___ = 100

88) 100 + ___ = 100

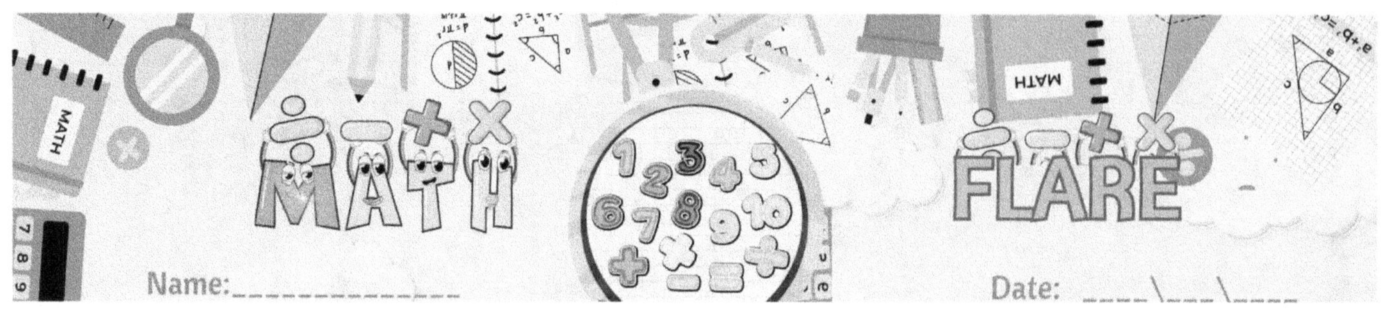

89) 38 + ___ = 100

90) 42 + ___ = 100

91) 70 + ___ = 100

92) 91 + __ = 100

93) 45 + ___ = 100

94) 35 + ___ = 100

95) 2 + ___ = 100

96) 56 + ___ = 100

97) 9 + ___ = 100

98) 99 + __ = 100

99) 49 + ___ = 100

100) 62 + ___ = 100

101) 60 + ___ = 100

102) 34 + ___ = 100

103) 38 + ___ = 100

104) 22 + ___ = 100

105) 21 + ___ = 100

106) 17 + ___ = 100

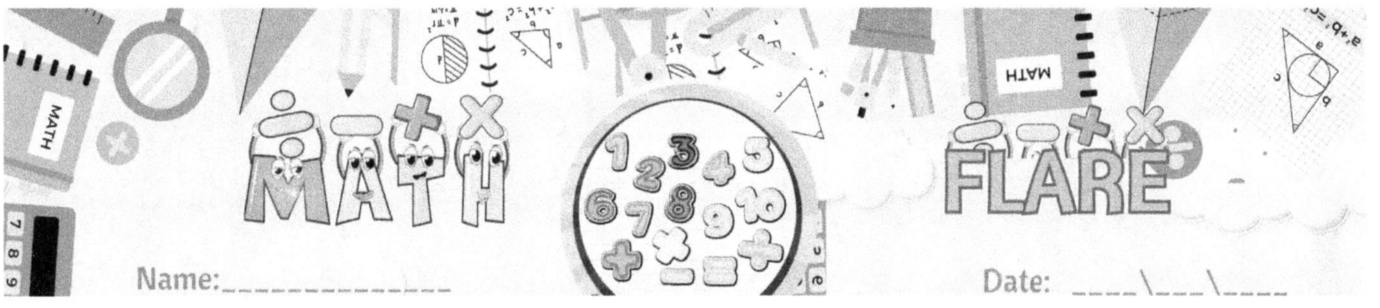

Addition: Unknown Number

Find the unknown number.

1) 63 + _37_ = 100

2) ____ + 54 = 146

3) 21 + 54 = ____

4) 89 + 52 = ____

5) ____ + 19 = 27

6) ____ + 59 = 65

7) 14 + 29 = ____

8) 22 + ____ = 99

9) 66 + 22 = ____

10) 65 + 97 = ____

11) 8 + 86 = ____

12) ____ + 53 = 124

13) 6 + 93 = ____

14) 31 + 88 = ____

15) 33 + 34 = ____

16) 27 + ____ = 38

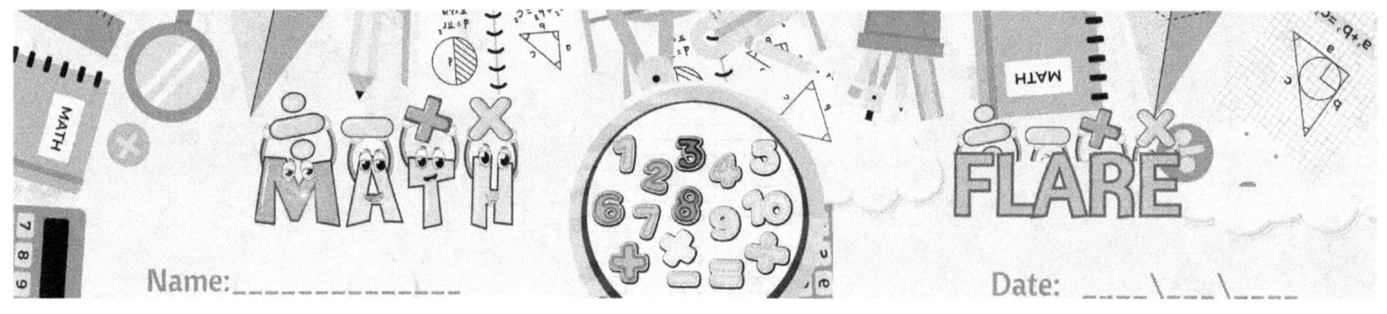

17) 94 + 53 = _____

18) 19 + 22 = _____

19) 97 + 38 = _____

20) 6 + _____ = 28

21) 30 + _____ = 37

22) _____ + 26 = 41

23) 31 + 91 = _____

24) 67 + 90 = _____

25) 83 + _____ = 165

26) 12 + _____ = 15

27) 9 + _____ = 92

28) 10 + _____ = 86

29) 66 + _____ = 106

30) 48 + 28 = _____

31) 24 + _____ = 26

32) 19 + 75 = _____

33) _____ + 96 = 188

34) 65 + _____ = 126

Name:____________________   Date: _____________

35) _____ + 100 = 111

36) 81 + 29 = _____

37) 17 + _____ = 61

38) 68 + _____ = 71

39) 73 + 46 = _____

40) 24 + 15 = _____

41) 26 + 41 = _____

42) 6 + _____ = 58

43) _____ + 26 = 49

44) _____ + 12 = 14

45) 45 + _____ = 87

46) _____ + 58 = 114

47) 90 + _____ = 168

48) 98 + 29 = _____

49) 87 + 40 = _____

50) 34 + _____ = 69

51) 27 + 8 = _____

52) _____ + 84 = 164

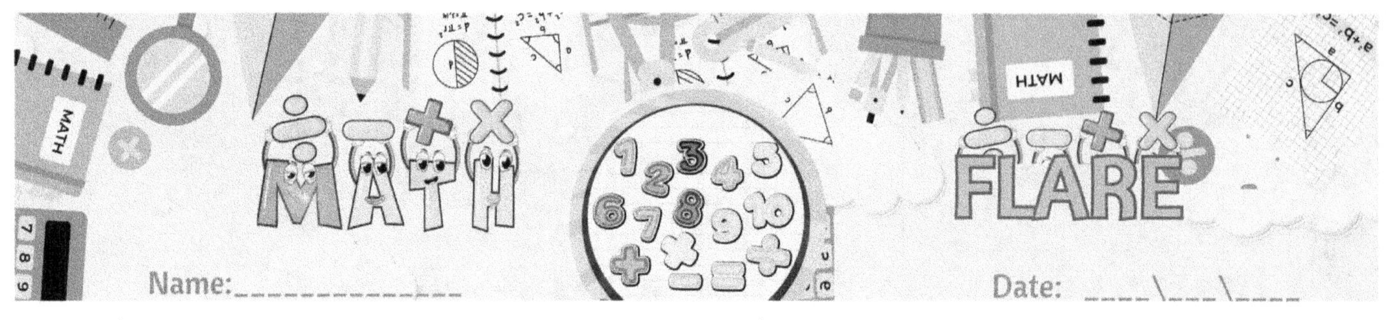

53) 2 + ____ = 86

54) 86 + 65 = ____

55) ____ + 8 = 24

56) 4 + ____ = 25

57) ____ + 34 = 51

58) ____ + 83 = 86

59) 96 + ____ = 164

60) 53 + ____ = 120

61) 94 + ____ = 148

62) ____ + 69 = 86

63) ____ + 24 = 69

64) ____ + 39 = 78

65) ____ + 40 = 86

66) ____ + 34 = 49

67) ____ + 89 = 102

68) ____ + 20 = 108

69) 61 + ____ = 83

70) ____ + 39 = 90

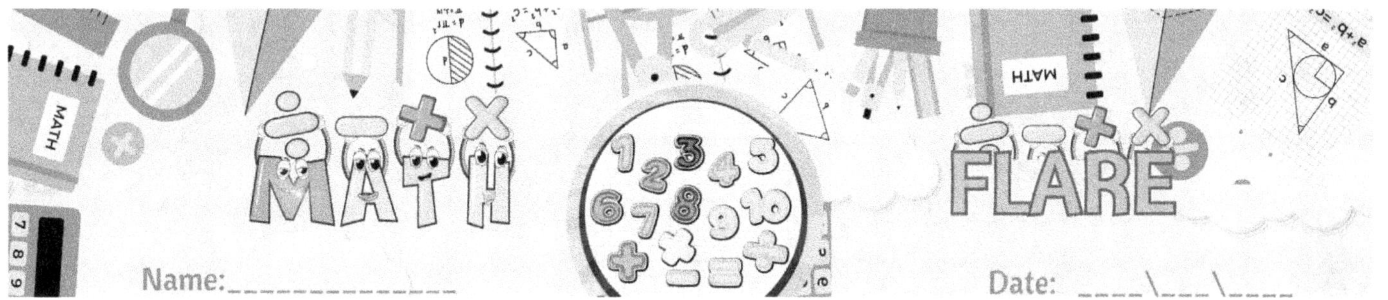

71) 40 + 37 = _____

72) 96 + _____ = 134

73) 39 + 36 = _____

74) _____ + 58 = 100

75) 76 + 16 = _____

76) 33 + 21 = _____

77) 87 + 67 = _____

78) 41 + _____ = 115

79) _____ + 13 = 103

80) 40 + _____ = 118

81) _____ + 48 = 94

82) 20 + 76 = _____

83) 93 + 70 = _____

84) _____ + 28 = 38

85) 45 + 84 = _____

86) _____ + 76 = 99

87) _____ + 15 = 33

88) _____ + 58 = 86

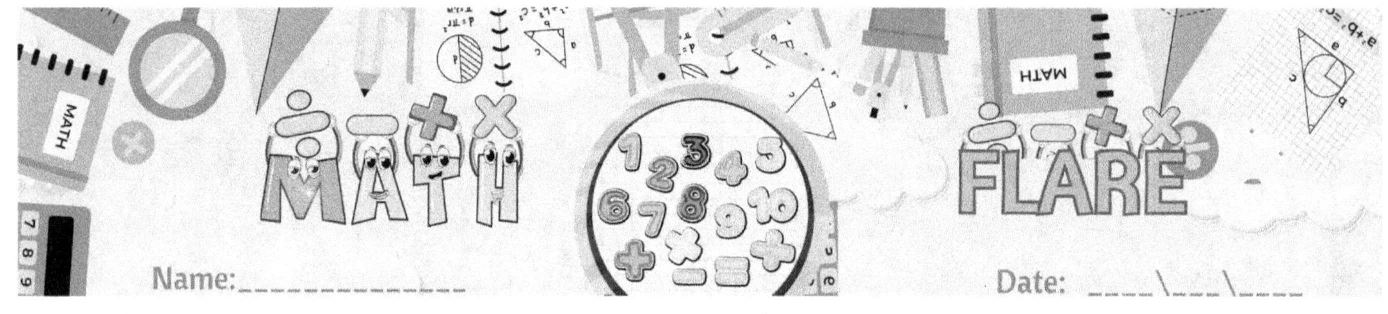

89) 58 + _____ = 138

90) 30 + 10 = _____

91) 82 + _____ = 163

92) 63 + _____ = 95

93) 9 + 95 = _____

94) 47 + _____ = 92

95) _____ + 16 = 65

96) 29 + _____ = 78

97) 82 + _____ = 155

98) 93 + 92 = _____

99) _____ + 21 = 40

100) 45 + _____ = 114

101) 27 + 15 = _____

102) _____ + 92 = 105

103) _____ + 57 = 150

104) 4 + 73 = _____

105) 40 + _____ = 123

106) 17 + _____ = 29

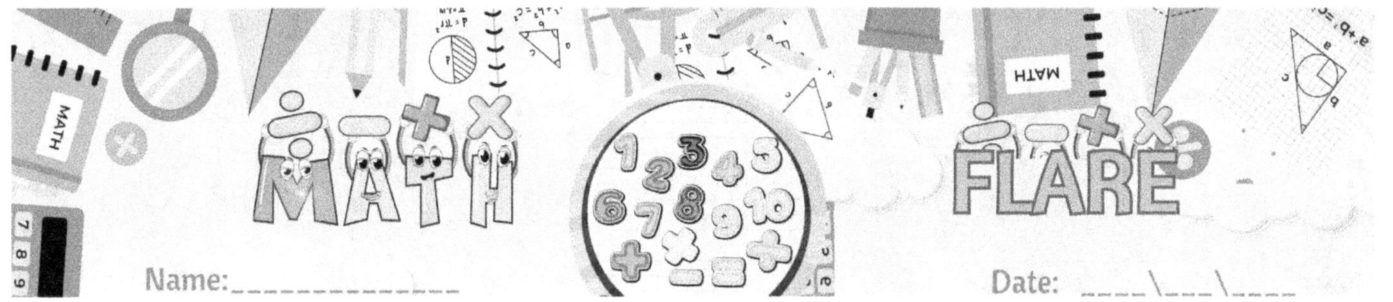

107) 82 + _____ = 113

108) 96 + _____ = 161

109) _____ + 88 = 172

110) _____ + 98 = 166

111) 24 + _____ = 89

112) 79 + 31 = _____

113) 56 + 74 = _____

114) 94 + 44 = _____

115) 22 + _____ = 58

116) 40 + 38 = _____

117) 36 + _____ = 97

118) 83 + 68 = _____

119) 69 + _____ = 141

120) 39 + 52 = _____

121) 92 + 75 = _____

122) 6 + 66 = _____

123) 99 + 18 = _____

124) 67 + _____ = 118

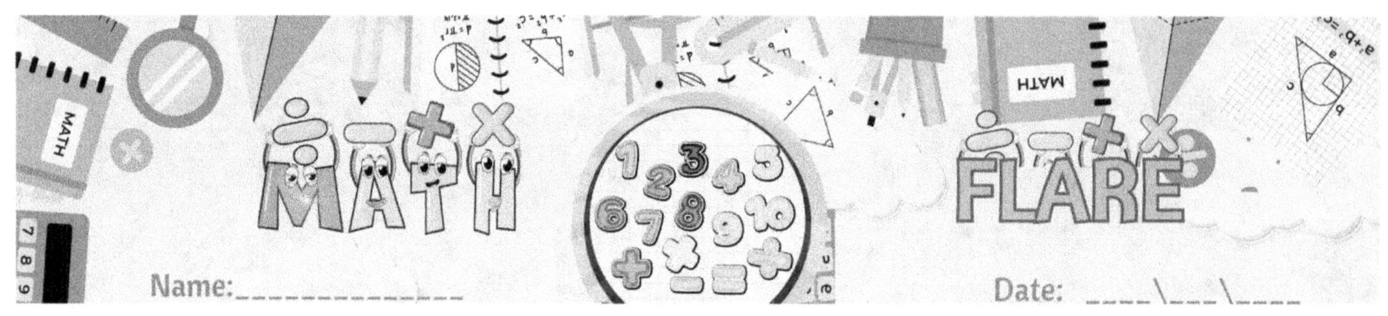

125) 78 + _____ = 107

126) 9 + _____ = 40

127) 52 + _____ = 99

128) 46 + _____ = 108

129) _____ + 82 = 118

130) _____ + 19 = 56

131) 63 + _____ = 123

132) 52 + 4 = _____

133) 44 + _____ = 123

134) 76 + _____ = 98

135) 96 + _____ = 110

136) 50 + 18 = _____

137) 7 + _____ = 57

138) _____ + 14 = 73

139) 32 + 38 = _____

140) 8 + _____ = 52

141) 67 + 93 = _____

142) 29 + 10 = _____

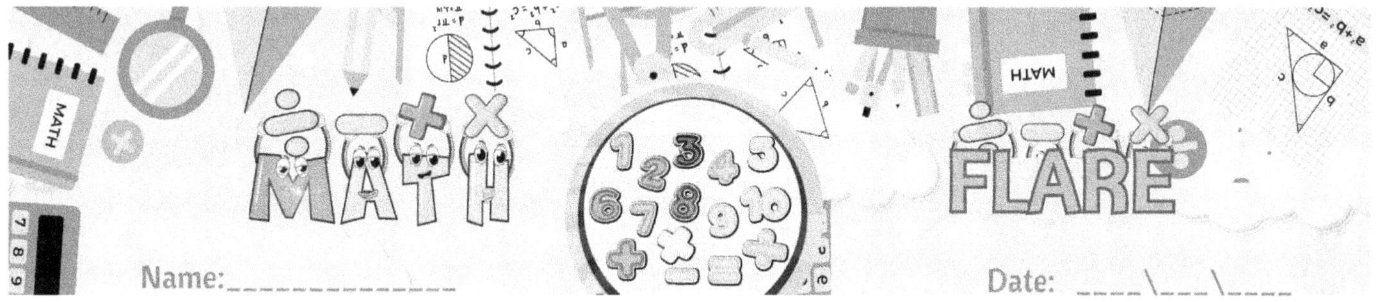

143) ____ + 89 = 174

144) ____ + 22 = 38

145) 33 + ____ = 120

146) 35 + 20 = ____

147) 89 + ____ = 122

148) ____ + 3 = 27

149) 23 + 21 = ____

150) ____ + 46 = 88

151) ____ + 50 = 55

152) 34 + ____ = 129

153) 80 + ____ = 116

154) ____ + 96 = 136

155) 4 + ____ = 27

156) 52 + 99 = ____

157) 12 + ____ = 32

158) 93 + 59 = ____

159) ____ + 35 = 111

160) 93 + 87 = ____

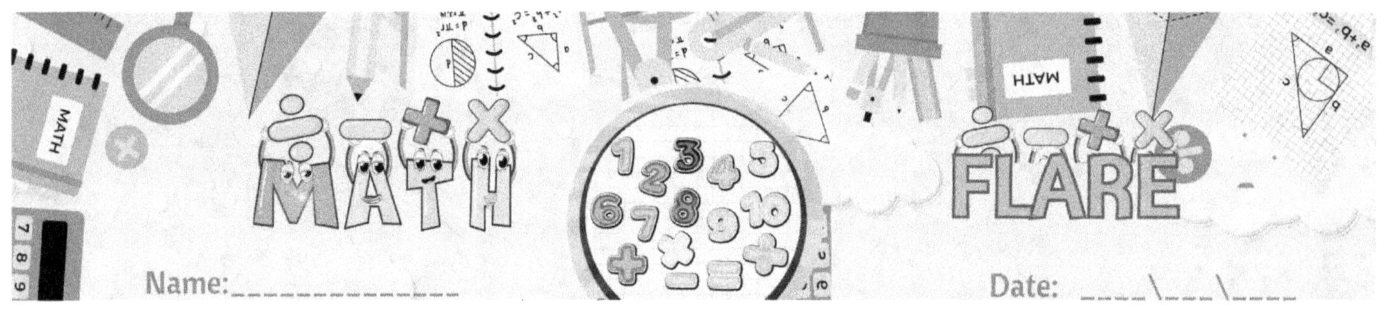

161) 6 + 27 = _____

162) 95 + 10 = _____

163) _____ + 31 = 109

164) 29 + 74 = _____

165) 27 + 57 = _____

166) 91 + _____ = 103

167) _____ + 62 = 158

168) _____ + 17 = 57

169) _____ + 34 = 94

170) 30 + _____ = 81

171) 50 + _____ = 70

172) 19 + _____ = 31

173) _____ + 36 = 72

174) 9 + 70 = _____

175) 40 + 65 = _____

176) _____ + 88 = 115

177) 28 + _____ = 84

178) 41 + _____ = 119

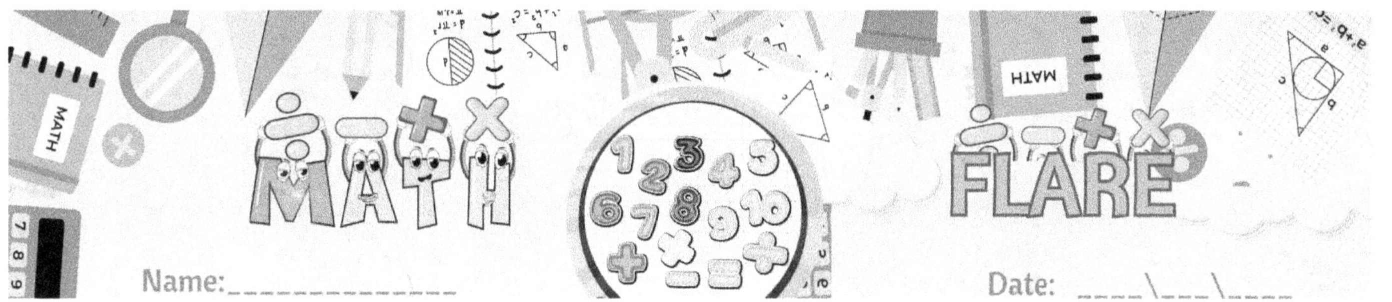

179) _____ + 25 = 80

180) 18 + _____ = 69

181) 8 + 66 = _____

182) 71 + _____ = 118

183) 31 + _____ = 72

184) 4 + 51 = _____

185) 80 + 77 = _____

186) 99 + 43 = _____

187) 6 + _____ = 50

188) _____ + 86 = 124

189) _____ + 85 = 93

190) 74 + 43 = _____

191) 23 + _____ = 83

192) 35 + 62 = _____

193) 31 + 5 = _____

194) 84 + 41 = _____

195) 21 + _____ = 83

196) _____ + 36 = 98

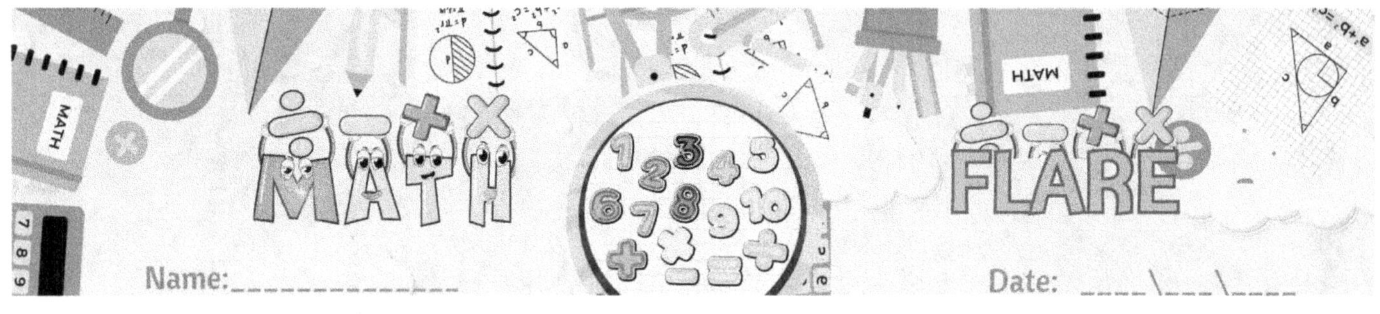

Subtraction: Unknown Number

Find the unknown number.

1) 25 - _20_ = 5

2) ____ - 41 = 8

3) 54 - ____ = 15

4) 82 - 78 = ____

5) 39 - ____ = 16

6) 91 - ____ = 33

7) 69 - 59 = ____

8) ____ - 71 = 13

9) 26 - ____ = 11

10) 73 - 51 = ____

11) 55 - ____ = 14

12) 35 - 17 = ____

13) ____ - 4 = 34

14) 24 - ____ = 17

15) ____ - 38 = 23

16) 37 - 7 = ____

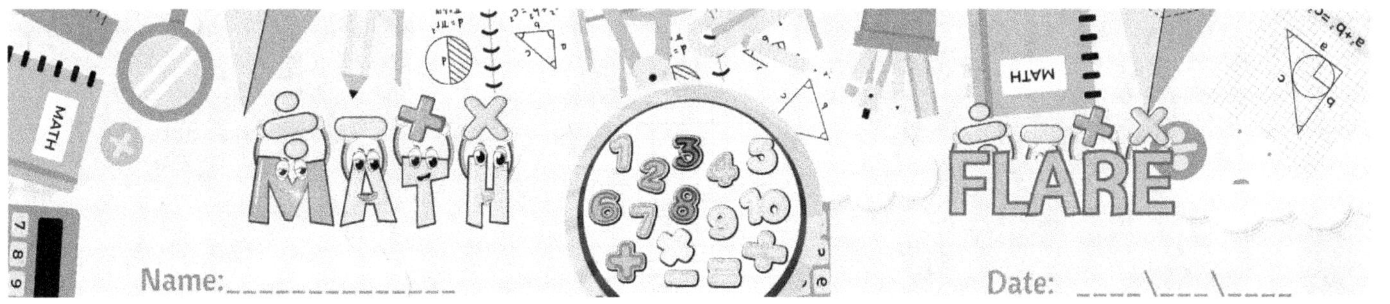

17) 23 - ____ = 8

18) 33 - 9 = ____

19) ____ - 53 = 47

20) 43 - ____ = 27

21) ____ - 11 = 3

22) ____ - 13 = 6

23) ____ - 53 = 20

24) 96 - 44 = ____

25) ____ - 29 = 0

26) ____ - 21 = 10

27) ____ - 84 = 8

28) 87 - ____ = 50

29) ____ - 54 = 2

30) 58 - 24 = ____

31) 61 - 33 = ____

32) 44 - ____ = 13

33) ____ - 25 = 10

34) 54 - 2 = ____

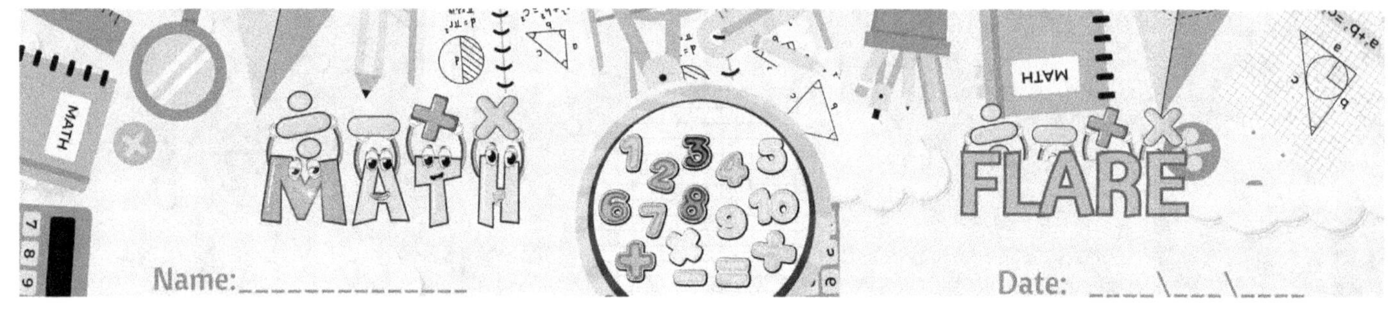

35) 63 - _____ = 27

36) _____ - 56 = 30

37) 26 - 10 = _____

38) _____ - 49 = 20

39) _____ - 44 = 24

40) 80 - _____ = 33

41) 22 - 16 = _____

42) _____ - 9 = 6

43) _____ - 29 = 16

44) _____ - 9 = 25

45) 80 - _____ = 13

46) 78 - _____ = 75

47) 99 - 96 = _____

48) 81 - 42 = _____

49) 48 - _____ = 29

50) 43 - _____ = 1

51) _____ - 29 = 2

52) _____ - 58 = 30

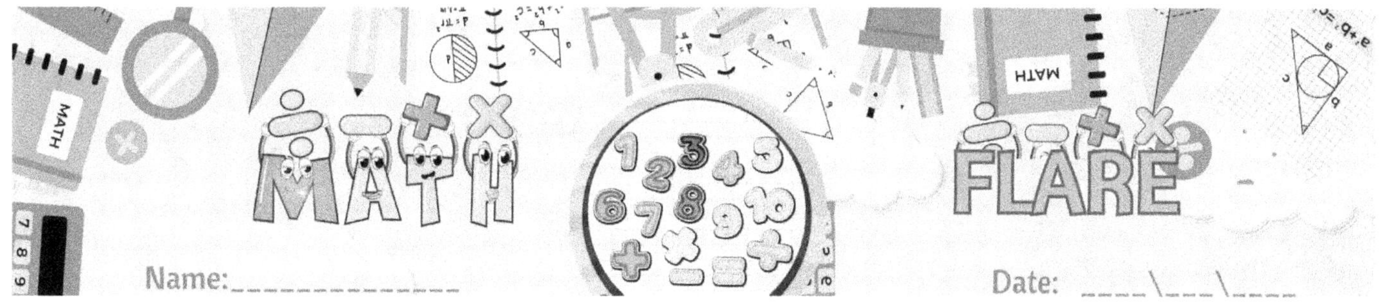

53) 24 - _____ = 10

54) _____ - 30 = 23

55) 34 - 6 = _____

56) 80 - _____ = 10

57) _____ - 26 = 1

58) 34 - 29 = _____

59) 52 - 42 = _____

60) 38 - _____ = 14

61) _____ - 14 = 36

62) _____ - 25 = 7

63) _____ - 67 = 15

64) 69 - 15 = _____

65) _____ - 9 = 52

66) 35 - 10 = _____

67) 34 - _____ = 7

68) 42 - _____ = 33

69) 86 - 35 = _____

70) 47 - 38 = _____

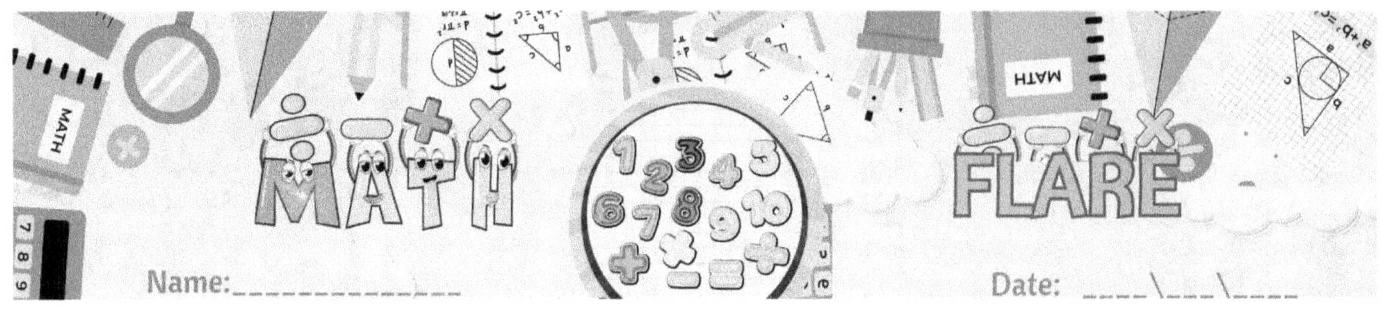

71) 25 - 18 = _____

72) _____ - 60 = 37

73) 15 - _____ = 2

74) 86 - 5 = _____

75) 74 - 69 = _____

76) 14 - 9 = _____

77) 17 - 13 = _____

78) _____ - 57 = 1

79) _____ - 8 = 65

80) 87 - _____ = 56

81) 93 - _____ = 67

82) _____ - 13 = 86

83) 89 - 46 = _____

84) 64 - 25 = _____

85) 63 - _____ = 57

86) 11 - 2 = _____

87) 46 - 23 = _____

88) _____ - 38 = 13

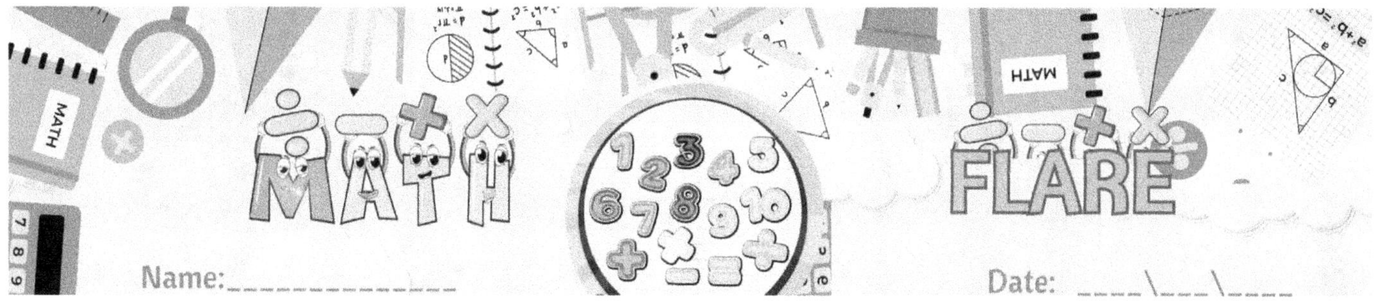

89) 36 - 23 = _____

90) _____ - 67 = 6

91) _____ - 36 = 19

92) _____ - 12 = 6

93) _____ - 14 = 12

94) 34 - 13 = _____

95) _____ - 5 = 55

96) 90 - _____ = 9

97) _____ - 63 = 12

98) 76 - _____ = 34

99) _____ - 17 = 19

100) 51 - 33 = _____

101) 92 - 91 = _____

102) _____ - 17 = 12

103) 35 - 28 = _____

104) 72 - _____ = 67

105) 46 - _____ = 3

106) 44 - 14 = _____

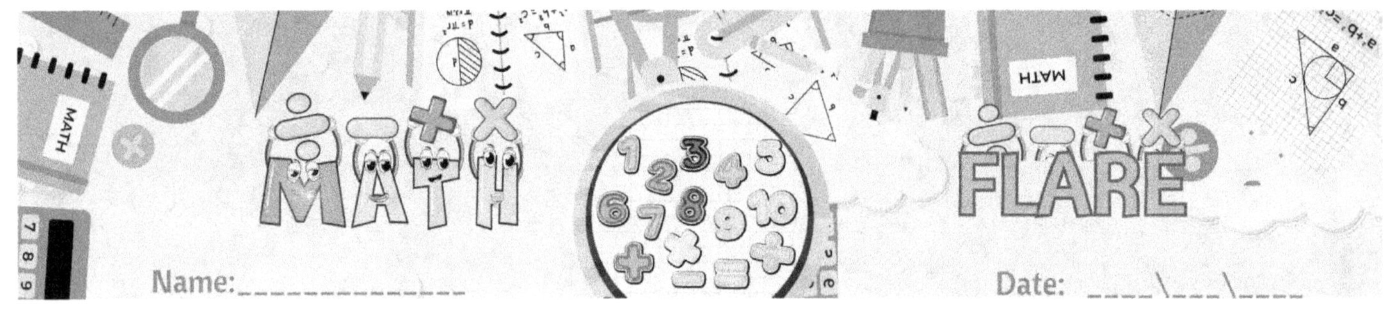

107) 80 - _____ = 52

108) 13 - 3 = _____

109) _____ - 4 = 36

110) 21 - 5 = _____

111) 62 - _____ = 44

112) _____ - 19 = 37

113) 64 - _____ = 27

114) _____ - 6 = 6

115) 91 - 15 = _____

116) _____ - 34 = 32

117) _____ - 21 = 3

118) _____ - 9 = 67

119) _____ - 31 = 20

120) 32 - _____ = 16

121) 72 - 32 = _____

122) 41 - _____ = 16

123) 72 - _____ = 30

124) 21 - 8 = _____

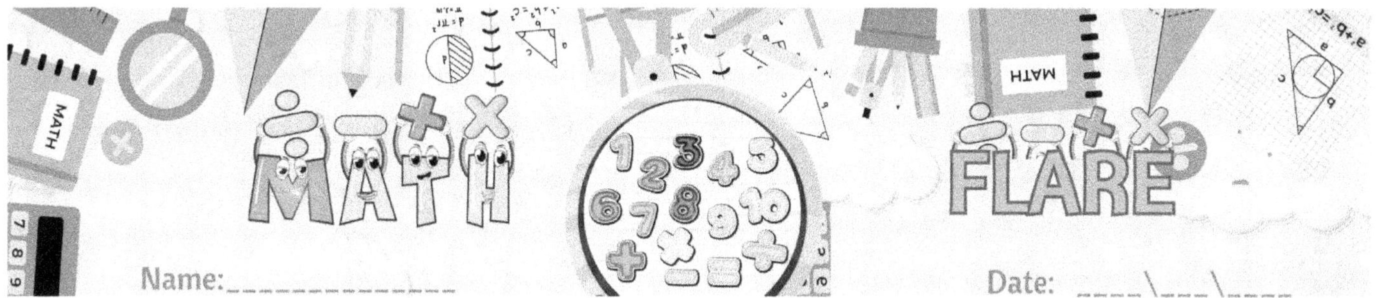

125) 82 - 44 = _____

126) 28 - 7 = _____

127) _____ - 10 = 30

128) 53 - 47 = _____

129) 98 - 70 = _____

130) _____ - 19 = 60

131) 25 - 7 = _____

132) 39 - _____ = 5

133) 24 - 22 = _____

134) 65 - _____ = 4

135) 77 - _____ = 20

136) _____ - 55 = 29

137) _____ - 9 = 48

138) 94 - _____ = 9

139) _____ - 3 = 64

140) 50 - 33 = _____

141) _____ - 25 = 43

142) _____ - 40 = 56

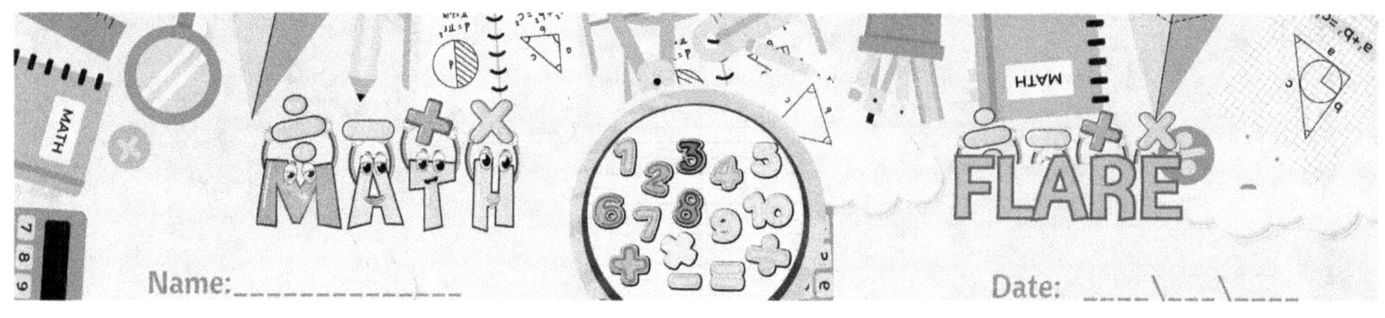

143) 25 - 23 = _____

144) _____ - 9 = 74

145) 66 - _____ = 28

146) 66 - 36 = _____

147) 73 - _____ = 39

148) _____ - 4 = 30

149) 36 - 29 = _____

150) 48 - 11 = _____

151) 79 - _____ = 11

152) 81 - 38 = _____

153) 45 - _____ = 14

154) 75 - 68 = _____

155) 74 - 43 = _____

156) 33 - _____ = 2

157) 34 - 5 = _____

158) _____ - 51 = 12

159) 36 - 33 = _____

160) 74 - _____ = 56

MathFlare - Math Workbook 2nd Grade

66

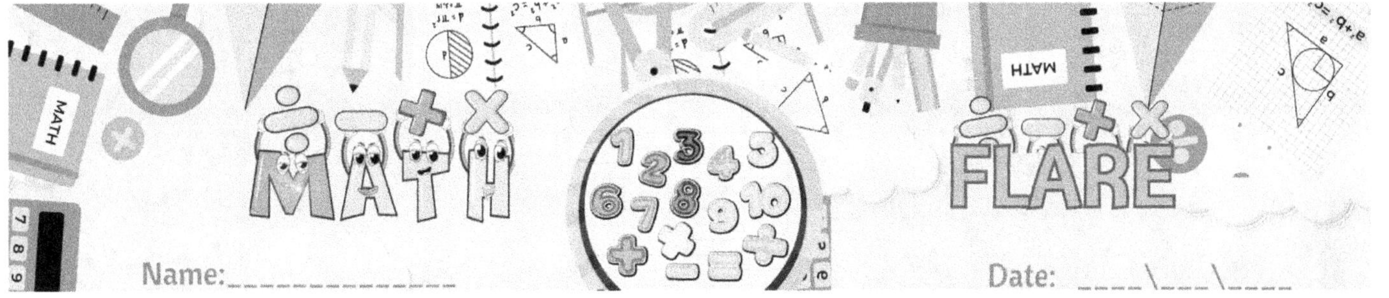

161) 19 - 10 = _____

162) 38 - _____ = 30

163) 20 - 6 = _____

164) 96 - 7 = _____

165) _____ - 74 = 15

166) _____ - 54 = 11

167) _____ - 16 = 48

168) _____ - 71 = 19

169) 62 - 31 = _____

170) 11 - 6 = _____

171) 28 - 26 = _____

172) 45 - 3 = _____

173) 39 - 26 = _____

174) 34 - _____ = 14

175) _____ - 42 = 47

176) 84 - _____ = 51

177) 19 - _____ = 15

178) 60 - _____ = 23

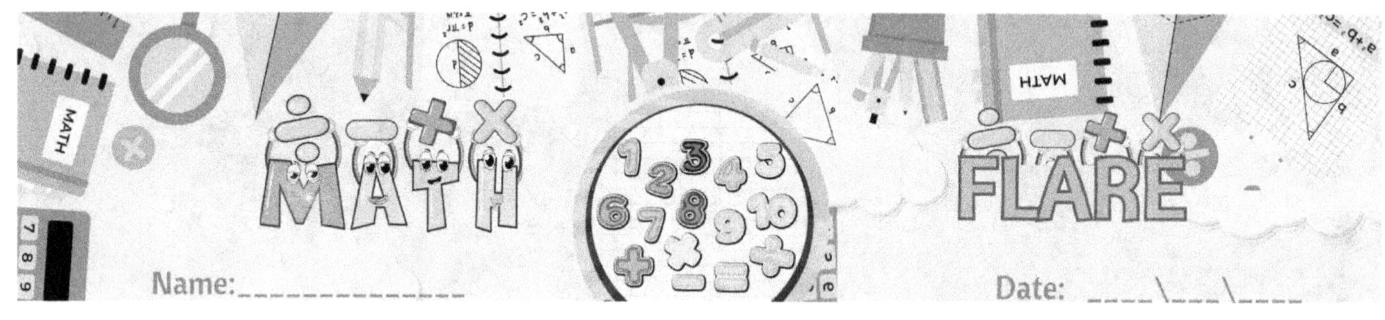

179) 42 - ____ = 37

180) 76 - 50 = ____

181) ____ - 11 = 1

182) 97 - 42 = ____

183) ____ - 2 = 40

184) 30 - 24 = ____

185) 91 - 22 = ____

186) 14 - 3 = ____

187) ____ - 7 = 15

188) ____ - 39 = 48

189) 12 - ____ = 7

190) ____ - 12 = 15

191) ____ - 3 = 8

192) ____ - 32 = 44

193) 22 - 14 = ____

194) 31 - 30 = ____

195) 23 - 21 = ____

196) 77 - ____ = 35

Addition Word Problems

1) Adalyn walked 7 miles yesterday and 20 miles today. How many miles did Adalyn walk in total?

$$
\begin{array}{r}
7 \quad \text{miles yesterday} \\
+\ 20 \quad \text{miles today} \\
\hline
27 \quad \text{Adalyn rode 27 miles in total}
\end{array}
$$

2) Thomas played 18 games of chess yesterday and 9 games today. How many games of chess did Thomas play in total?

3) Audrey has 14 knives. She gets 8 more knives. How many knives does Audrey have now?

4) Olivia has 8 gloves in a bag. If Olivia adds 17 more gloves to the bag, how many gloves does Olivia have in total?

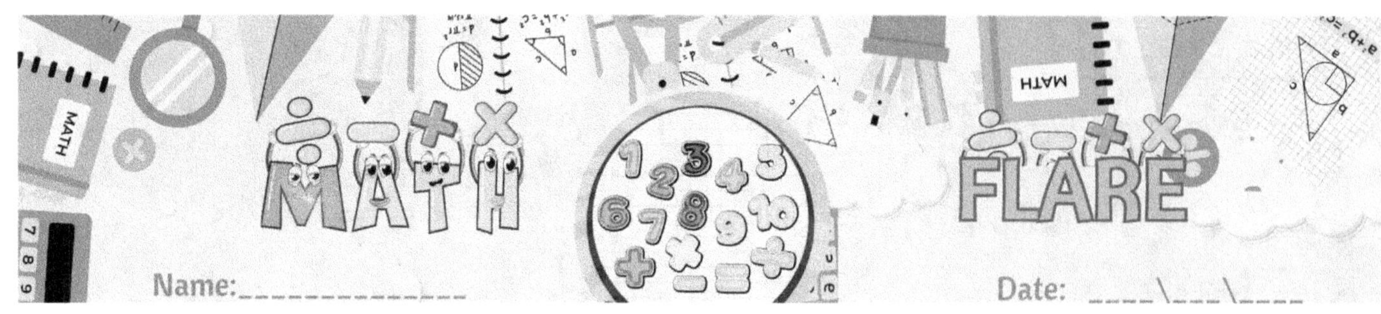

5) William has 2 shampoos. He finds 13 more shampoos. How many shampoos does he have now?

6) There are 19 vitamins in the room. 20 more vitamins are brought in. How many vitamins are in the room now?

7) Mason baked 13 cookies and 7 cupcakes. How many desserts did Mason bake in total?

8) There is 1 crows on a tree. 7 more crows land on the tree. How many crows are on the tree now?

Name:________________ Date: ____________

9) Mila has 14 rulers. She buys 16 more rulers at the store. How many rulers does Mila have now?

10) Emilia has 6 gauzes. Her friend gives her 18 more gauzes. How many gauzes does Emilia have now?

11) Cooper spent 11 dollars on Monday and 4 dollars on Tuesday. How much money did Cooper spend in total?

12) Piper bought pizzas with 2 slices. Later, Piper bought some more pizzas with 7 slices. How many slices of pizzas does Piper have in total?

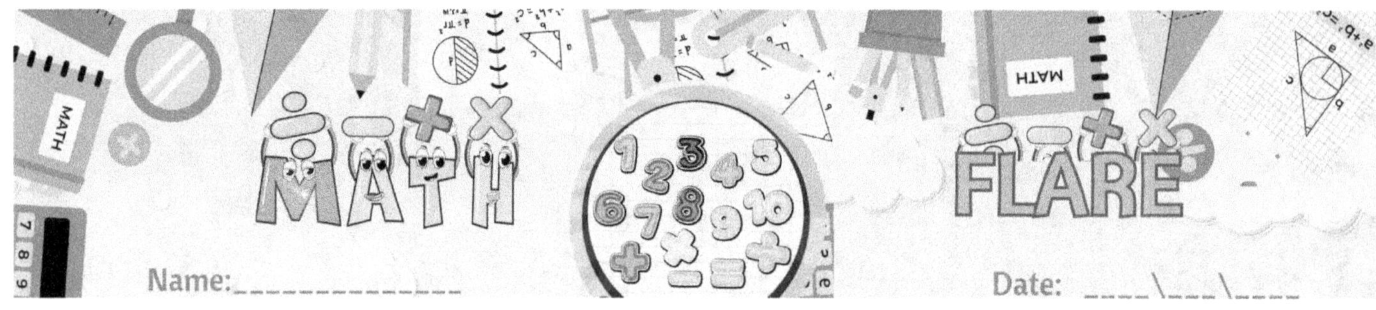

13) Brody has 1 perfume. His sister gives him 2 more perfumes .
How many perfumes does Brody have now?

14) Yesterday, Jade earned $11, and today, Jade earned $13. How
much money did Jade earn in total?

15) A machine has 15 parts. If 13 more parts are added, how many
parts does the machine have now?

16) Parker has 1 piano. He buys 6 more pianos. How many pianos
does she have now?

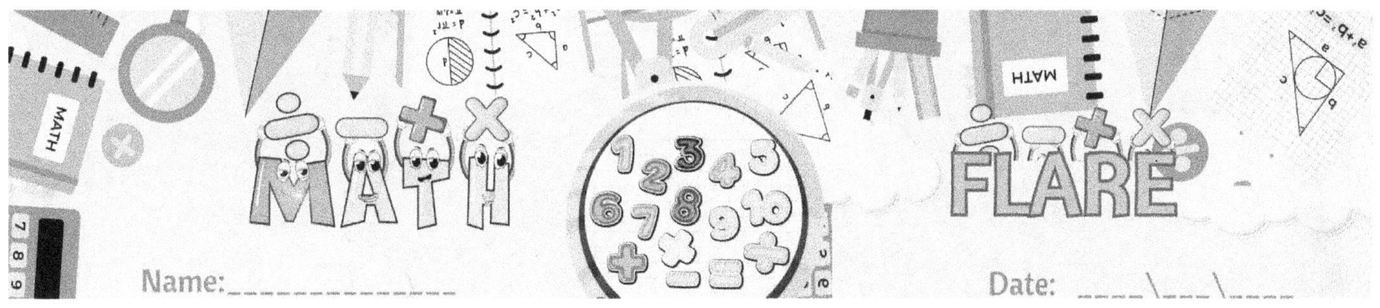

17) Levi has 9 fish in an aquarium. If Levi adds 11 more fish to the aquarium, how many fish will be in the aquarium in total?

18) Chloe baked 6 cakes yesterday and 12 cakes today. How many cakes did Chloe bake in total?

19) An object has 13 parts. If 19 more parts are added, how many parts does the object have now?

20) Ian has 5 red marbles and 19 blue marbles in a jar. How many marbles does Ian have in total?

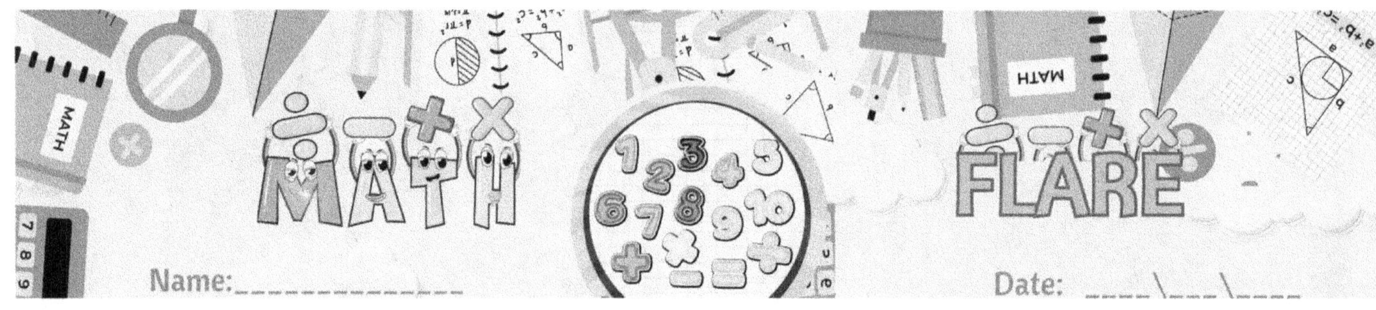

21) The weight of an empty container is 13 pounds. If the container is filled with 5 pounds of chocolates, what is the total weight of the container and its contents?

22) Wyatt has 15 dollars and found 6 more dollars on the ground. How much money does Wyatt have now?

23) Alexander made 20 cookies and Willow made 2 cookies. How many cookies were made in total?

24) There were 12 people in line at the store. After 6 more people joined the line, how many people are in the line now?

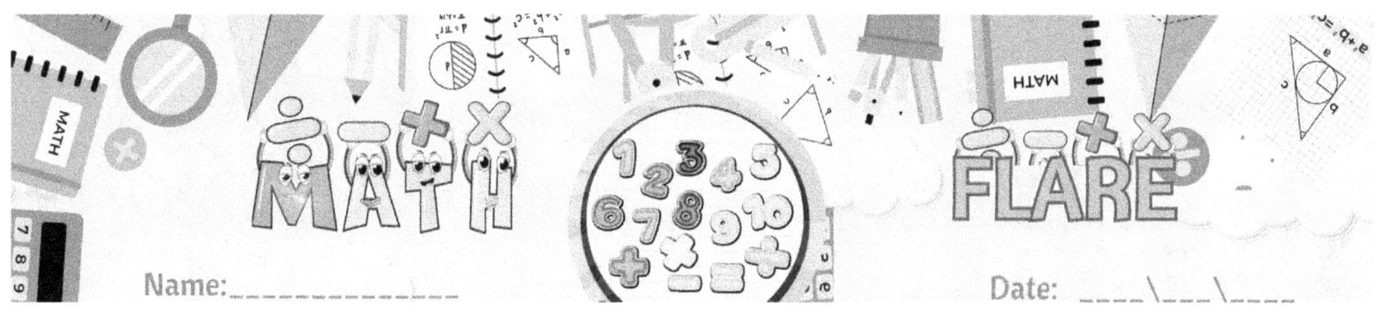

25) Xavier has a basket with 1 candy in it. After buying 18 more candies, how many candies does Xavier have in total?

26) Addison planted 12 flowers in the morning and 20 flowers in the afternoon. How many flowers did Addison plant?

27) Nicholas bought a bag of rocks for 9 dollars. Later, Nicholas bought another bag of rocks for 2 dollars. How much money did Nicholas spend in total?

28) A company produced 2 mirrors on Monday and 3 mirrors on Tuesday. How many mirrors did the company produce in total?

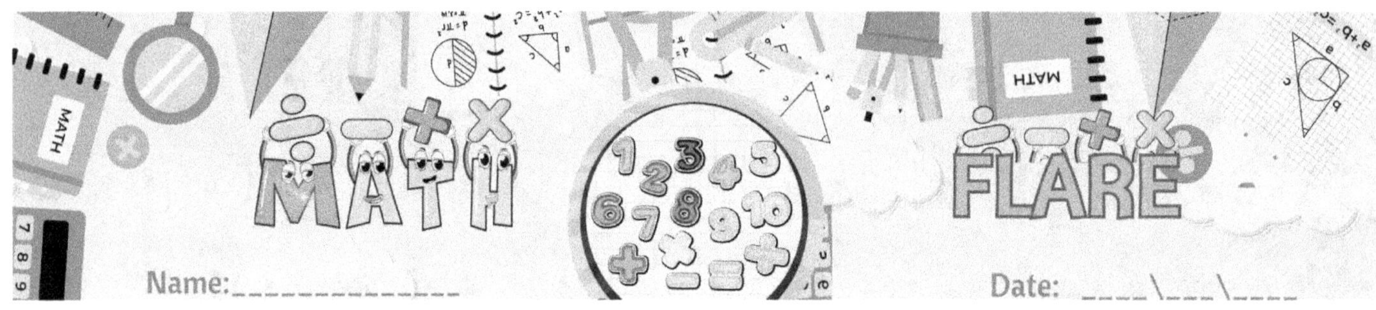

29) Isaac has 18 cameras and buys 11 more cameras. How many cameras does Isaac have in total?

30) Nova has 9 erasers. She gets 13 erasers from her friend. How many erasers does Nova have now?

31) A bus made 18 stops in the morning and 16 stops in the afternoon. How many stops did the bus make in total?

32) Jordyn wrote 3 pages of her book yesterday and 10 pages today. How many pages did she write in total?

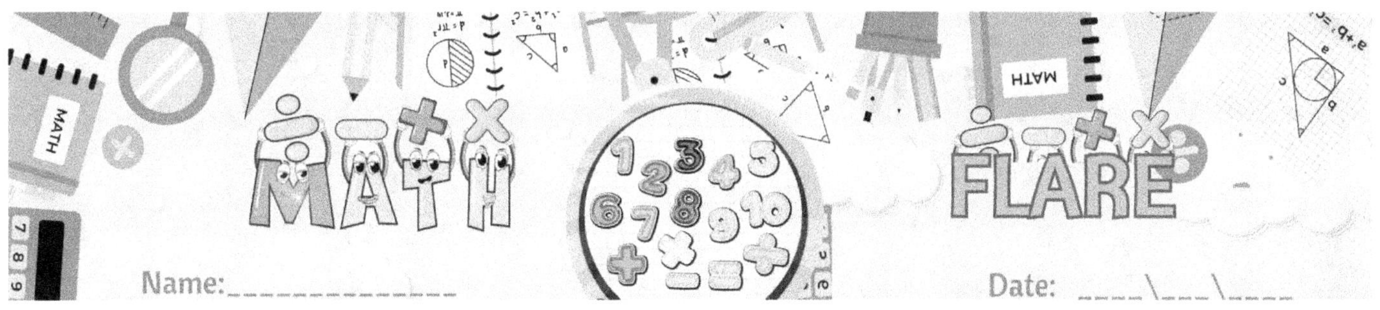

33) Roman drove 13 miles in the morning and 14 miles in the evening. How many miles did Roman drive in total?

34) Samuel has 12 apples and 3 oranges in a basket. How many fruits does Samuel have in total?

35) There is 1 cats in the ground. 10 more cats come to play. How many cats are in the ground now?

36) Adam had 15 dollars and earned 15 more dollars. How much money does Adam have now?

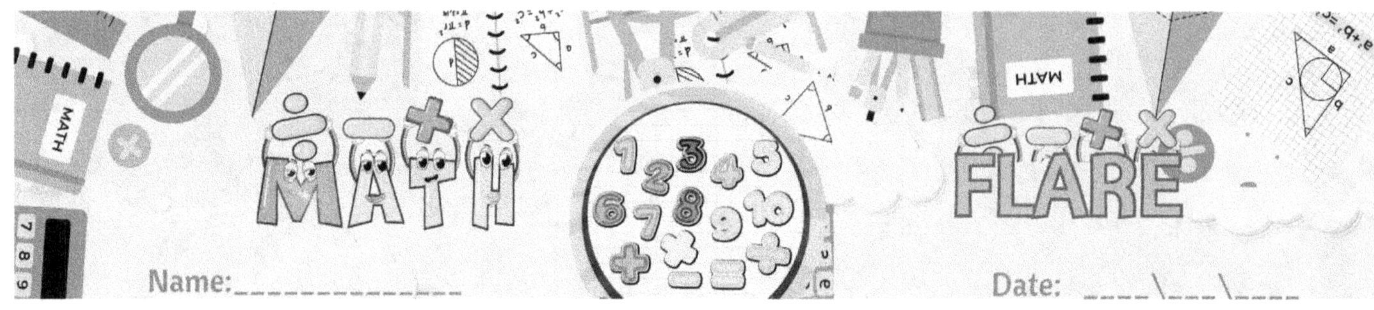

37) There are 11 fishes in the pond. 7 more fishes join them. How many fishes are in the pond now?

38) Maria watched 5 movies last week and 7 movies this week. How many movies did Maria watch altogether?

39) Isaac has 10 carrots. He gets 17 more carrots as a gift. How many carrots does Isaac have now?

40) Lucas has 8 red medicines and 19 green medicines. If Lucas puts all the medicines in a basket, how many medicines are in the basket in total?

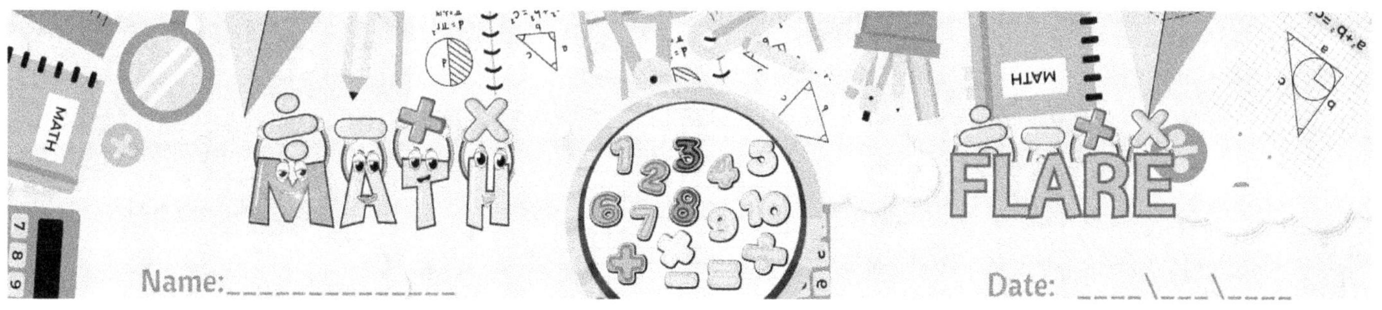

Subtraction Word Problems

1) Emma and Sharon had 5 maps altogether. Sharon gave 3 maps to Billy. How many maps do they have left?

$$5 \quad \text{Emma and Sharon have 5 maps}$$
$$- \, 3 \quad \underline{\text{Sharon Gave 3 maps to Billy}}$$
$$2 \quad \text{they have 2 maps left}$$

2) A recipe needs 9 cups of sugar. Janet added 1 cups of sugar. How many cups of sugar are still needed?

3) Amy has 4 dollars. She wants to buy forks, which costs 9 dollars. How much more money does she need to buy it?

4) Sharon baked a 2 cookies. 1 of them were chocolate chip cookies and the rest were oatmeal raisin cookies. How many oatmeal raisin cookies did Sharon bake?

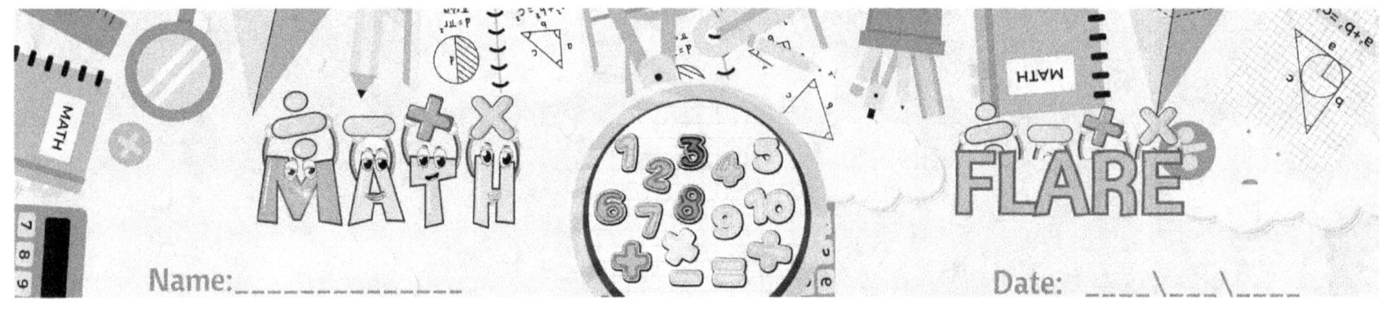

5) A cake recipe calls for 6 cups of flour. 1 cups of flour have already been added. How many more cups of flour are needed?

6) Jessica bought scarves for 9 dollars. She later returned some scarves and received a refund of 3 dollars. How much money did she end up spending on scarves?

7) Deborah wants to buy syringes, which costs 7 dollars. She has 4 dollars and plans to save the rest. How much more money does she need to save to buy syringes?

8) There are 5 cars in a parking lot. Andrew took 3 cars out of the lot. How many cars are still in the lot?

9) There are 2 fish in a pond. Jennifer caught 1 fish. How many fish are left in the pond?

10) William has 2 dollars. He needs to buy toothbrushes that costs 2 dollars. How much money will he have left after buying the toothbrushes?

11) Matthew had 7 dollars. He spent 2 dollars on a chocolates. How much money does Matthew have left?

12) Paul has 5 dollars. He wants to buy knives that costs 4 dollars. How much more money does he need to buy the knives?

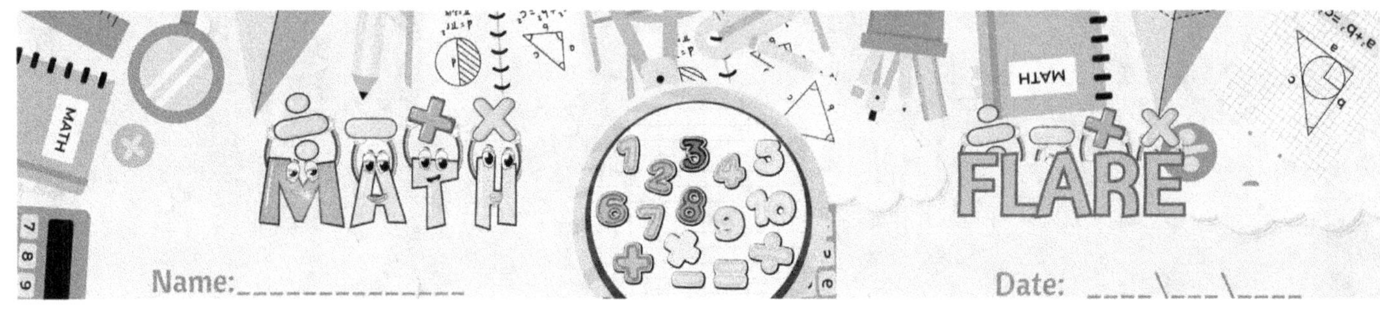

13) A pizza has 2 slices. Sandra ate 1 slices. How many slices of pizza are left?

14) There are 6 turtles in a pond. If 2 leave, how many turtles are left in the pond?

15) Scalpels originally cost 7 dollars, but it is now on sale for 6 dollars. How much money can you save by buying it on sale?

16) There are 7 fish in a tank. If 7 leave, how many fish are left in the tank?

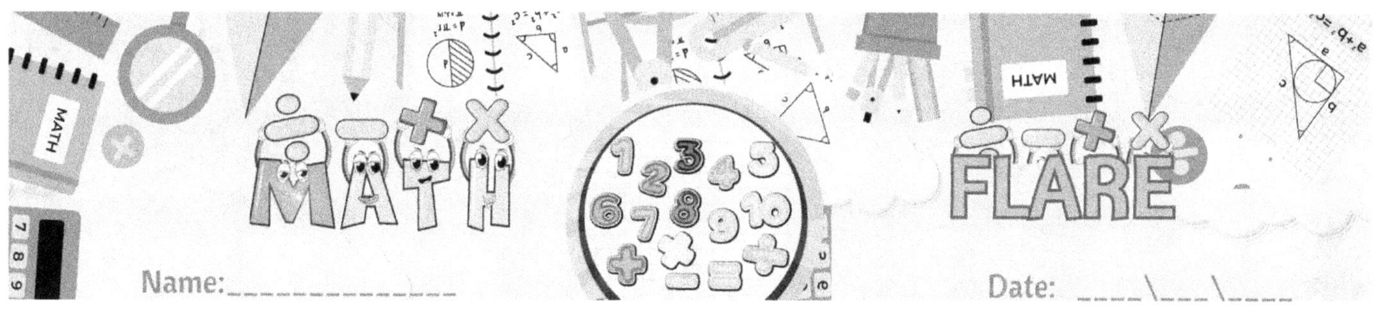

Name:________________   Date: ______________

17) Karen bought pants for 3 dollars but later found out it was on sale for 1 dollars less. How much did she overpay for pants?

18) A box of stethoscopes weighs 3 pounds. If you remove 1 pounds from it, how much does it weigh now?

19) There are 5 dogs in a park. If 5 leave, how many dogs are left in the park?

20) Janet and Sharon went on a shopping spree and bought 1 camera. After returning home, they realized that they didn't need 1 of them. How many cameras did they end up keeping?

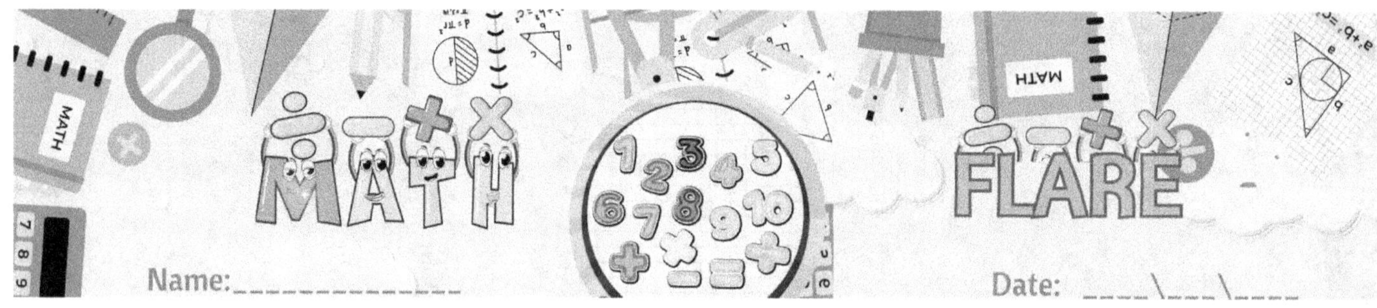

21) A folders costs $7 and a pen costs $4. How much more expensive is the folders than the pen?

22) There were 7 students in a class. 5 of them were absent. How many students were present in the class?

23) Anthony saved up 9 dollars to buy gauzes. He spent 5 dollars on it. How much money does he have left?

24) There are 5 mirrors in a bag. Michele took 4 mirrors out of the bag. How many mirrors are still in the bag?

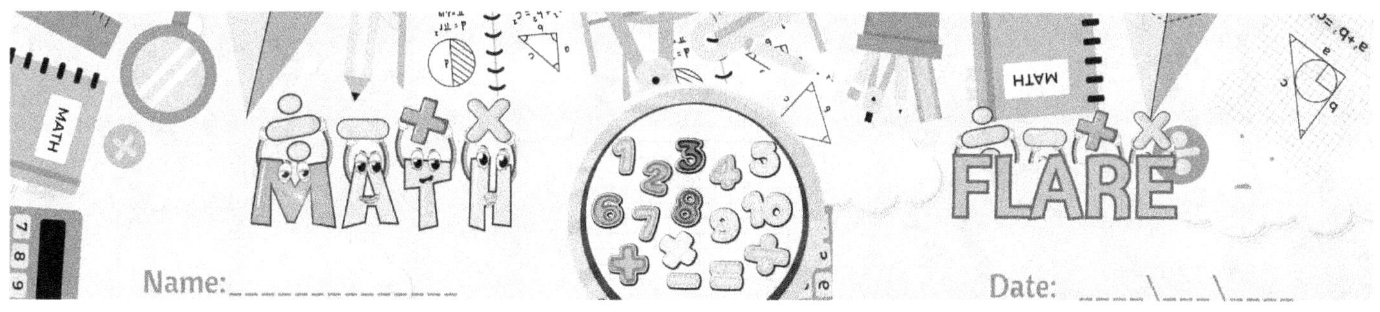

25) Sharon has 9 tables in her collection. She gave 5 of them to her friend. How many tables does Sharon have now?

26) Nicholas has 3 red shirts and 1 green shirt. How many more red shirts does Nicholas have than green shirts?

27) Jennifer has 8 bananas. She gave 5 bananas to Amy. How many bananas does Jennifer have now?

28) If you have 6 towels and you give away 4, how many towels do you have left?

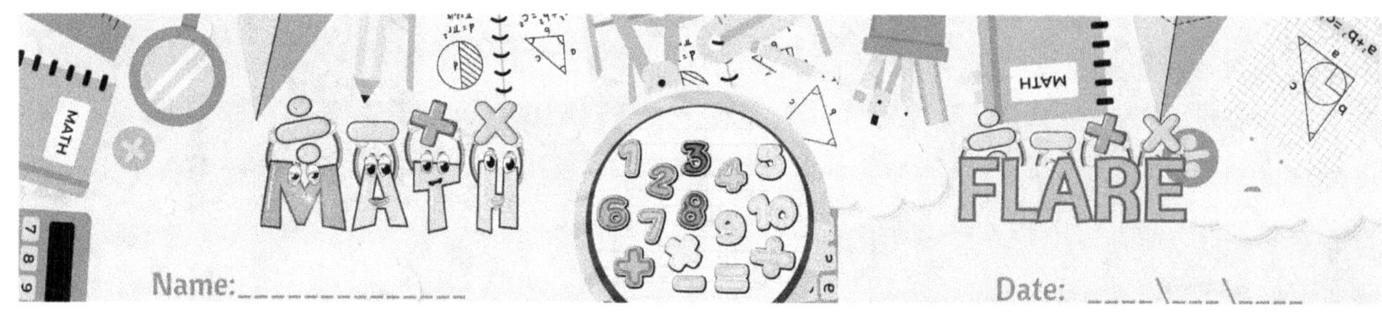

29) There are 6 surgical masks. 6 surgical masks are blue and the rest are red. How many red surgical masks are in the box?

30) Karen had 2 dollars. She spent 1 dollars on thermometer. How much money does Karen have left?

31) Barbara bought gloves for 7 dollars. She received 5 dollars in change. How much did gloves cost?

32) Joseph has 3 gloves in his collection. He sold 1 of them at a sale. How many gloves does he have left in his collection?

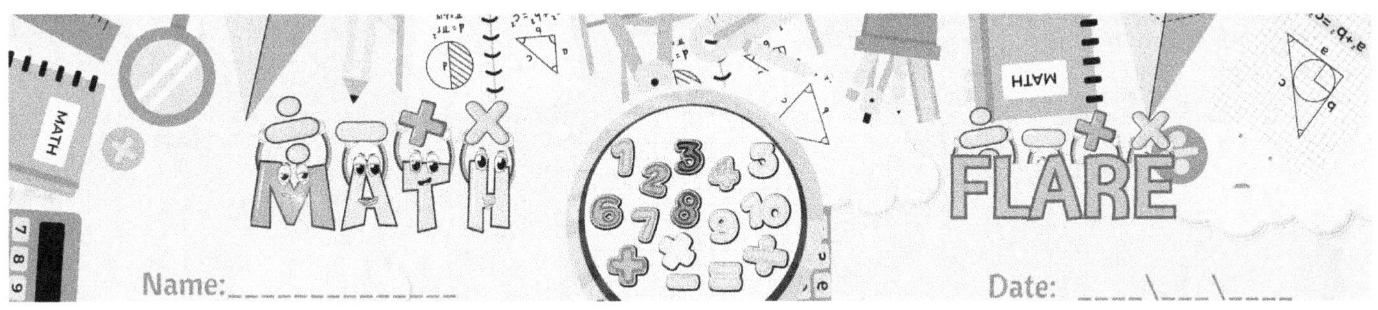

33) Jennifer has 8 radios. She lost 4 of them. How many radios does Jennifer have left?

34) Christopher is 3 years old and Ryan is 1 years old. What is the difference in their ages?

35) A cake recipe requires 5 cups of sugar. Susan only has 4 cups of sugar. How many more cups of sugar does Susan need?

36) A box had 4 chocolates. Deborah ate 1 chocolates. How many chocolates are left in the box?

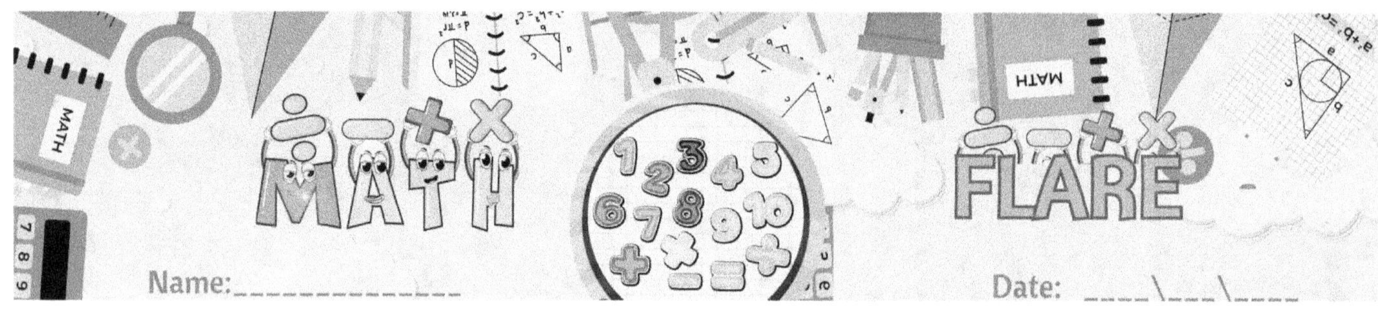

37) Steven has 7 bandages. He traded 2 of them with his friend. How many bandages does Steven have now?

38) A small bag of chips has 7 chips in it. Adam ate 2 chips. How many chips are left in the bag?

39) Spoons costs 7 dollars. If you paid $6. How much change will you get back?

40) Anthony had 10 soaps. He gave 10 soaps to Amanda. How many soaps does Anthony have left?

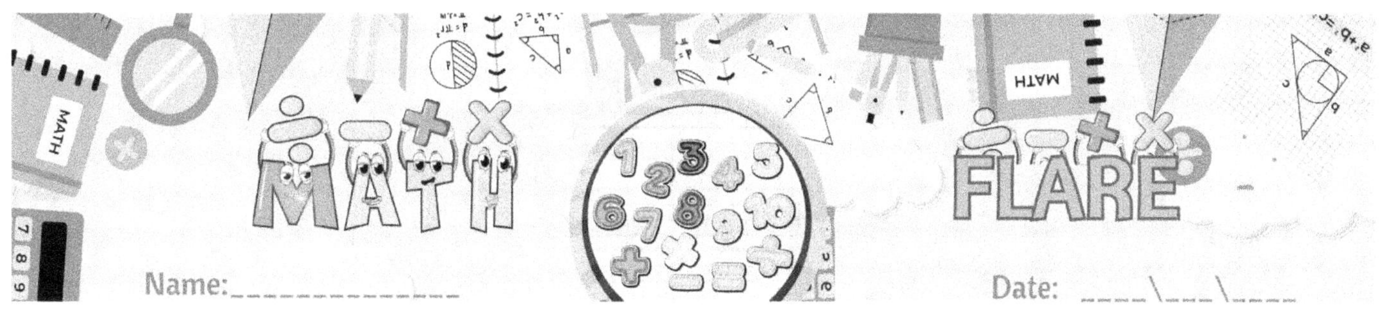

41) If plates costs 8 dollars and you have 8 dollars, how much more money do you need to buy it?

42) A pack of gum had 4 pieces. Elizabeth took 3 pieces of gum. How many pieces of gum are left in the pack?

43) Jackie and Stephanie went shopping for books. They had 2 dollars to spend but 1 dollars ended up being spent. How much money do they have left?

44) Janet and Linda went shopping for cups. They had 4 dollars to spend but 4 dollars ended up being spent. How much money do they have left?

Chapter. 02

Multiplication

Multiplication

Multiplication is an easy way of adding numbers together quickly. Instead of adding the same number repeatedly, we use multiplication to find the total much faster.

For instance, rather than adding 2 + 2 + 2 + 2 + 2, we can multiply 2 by 5 to get the same result: 2 x 5 = 10.

Here, the first number (2) is called the multiplicand, second number (5) is the multiplier. The answer we get, in this case, 10, is called the product.

Let's think of multiplication as repeated addition.

Take 2 x 5, for example. It means adding 2 together five times, which we can illustrate as: 2 + 2 + 2 + 2 + 2 = 10

Multiplication can also be visualized as groups of objects. Imagine we have 2 groups, each containing 5 oranges.

To find the total number of oranges, we multiply the number of groups (2) by the number of oranges in each group (5):

2 groups of 5 oranges = 10 oranges

Expressed as multiplication: 2 x 5 = 10

In summary, multiplication offers various ways to approach it: through repeated addition or by envisioning groups of objects. It's a powerful tool that makes solving math problems much quicker and more efficient!

We can also use the following table to quickly remember multiplication facts. The intersection of two points shows the product of two numbers.

For instance, the product of **5 x 6 = 30, or 6 x 5 = 30.**

	1	2	3	4	5	6	7	8	9	10
1	1	2	3	4	5	6	7	8	9	10
2	2	4	6	8	10	12	14	16	18	20
3	3	6	9	12	15	18	21	24	27	30
4	4	8	12	16	20	24	28	32	36	40
5	5	10	15	20	25	30	35	40	45	50
6	6	12	18	24	30	36	42	48	54	60
7	7	14	21	28	35	42	49	56	63	70
8	8	16	24	32	40	48	56	64	72	80
9	9	18	27	36	45	54	63	72	81	90
10	10	20	30	40	50	60	70	80	90	100

Commutative Property of Multiplication

The commutative property of multiplication is a special rule in math that tells us the order of the numbers being multiplied doesn't affect the result.

For instance, let's take 2 x 5. If we switch the order of the numbers, multiplying 5 by 2 instead, we'll still end up with the same answer: 2 x 5 = 10, or 5 x 2 = 10.

So, whether we multiply 2 by 5 or 5 by 2, we get 10. That's the commutative property of multiplication in action!

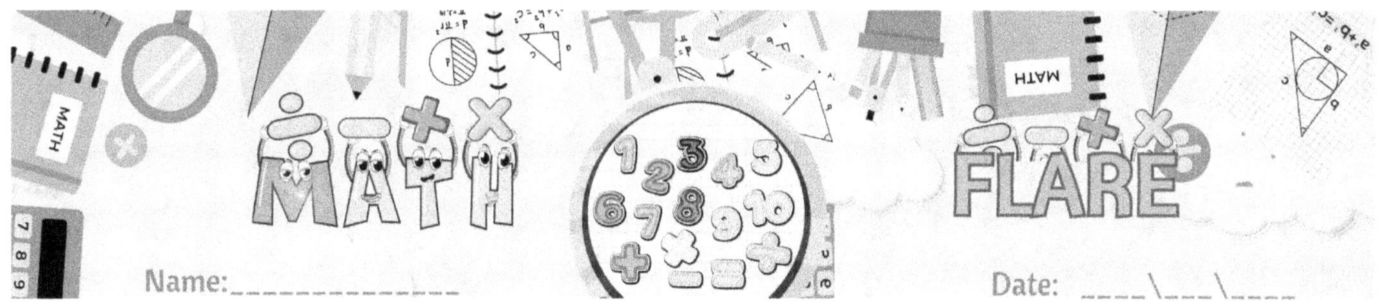

Multiplication by 1

1) 6
   × 1
   ───
    6

2) 7
   × 1
   ───
    7

3) 1
   × 1
   ───

4) 1
   × 9
   ───

5) 1
   × 8
   ───

6) 1
   × 4
   ───

7) 2
   × 1
   ───

8) 1
   × 5
   ───

9) 1
   × 3
   ───

10) 4
    × 1
    ───

11) 5
    × 1
    ───

12) 8
    × 1
    ───

13) 9
    × 1
    ───

14) 1
    × 2
    ───

15) 1
    × 6
    ───

16) 3
    × 1
    ───

17) 1
    × 7
    ───

18) 1
    × 3
    ───

19) 2
    × 1
    ───

20) 8
    × 1
    ───

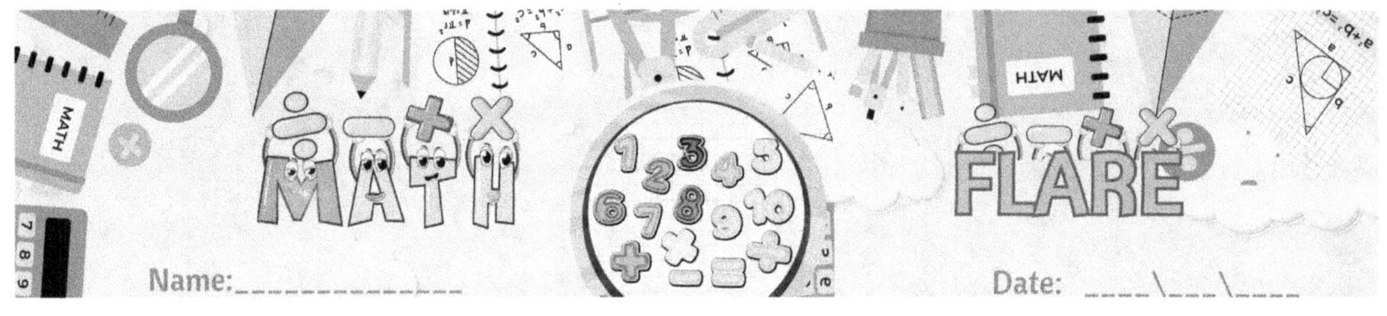

Multiplication by 2

1) $\begin{array}{r} 2 \\ \times\ 6 \\ \hline \end{array}$

2) $\begin{array}{r} 2 \\ \times\ 8 \\ \hline \end{array}$

3) $\begin{array}{r} 2 \\ \times\ 7 \\ \hline \end{array}$

4) $\begin{array}{r} 3 \\ \times\ 2 \\ \hline \end{array}$

5) $\begin{array}{r} 4 \\ \times\ 2 \\ \hline \end{array}$

6) $\begin{array}{r} 2 \\ \times\ 2 \\ \hline \end{array}$

7) $\begin{array}{r} 5 \\ \times\ 2 \\ \hline \end{array}$

8) $\begin{array}{r} 1 \\ \times\ 2 \\ \hline \end{array}$

9) $\begin{array}{r} 9 \\ \times\ 2 \\ \hline \end{array}$

10) $\begin{array}{r} 8 \\ \times\ 2 \\ \hline \end{array}$

11) $\begin{array}{r} 2 \\ \times\ 4 \\ \hline \end{array}$

12) $\begin{array}{r} 2 \\ \times\ 3 \\ \hline \end{array}$

13) $\begin{array}{r} 7 \\ \times\ 2 \\ \hline \end{array}$

14) $\begin{array}{r} 2 \\ \times\ 5 \\ \hline \end{array}$

15) $\begin{array}{r} 6 \\ \times\ 2 \\ \hline \end{array}$

16) $\begin{array}{r} 2 \\ \times\ 1 \\ \hline \end{array}$

17) $\begin{array}{r} 2 \\ \times\ 9 \\ \hline \end{array}$

18) $\begin{array}{r} 2 \\ \times\ 1 \\ \hline \end{array}$

19) $\begin{array}{r} 1 \\ \times\ 2 \\ \hline \end{array}$

20) $\begin{array}{r} 6 \\ \times\ 2 \\ \hline \end{array}$

Multiplication by 3

1) 3
  × 3

2) 3
  × 7

3) 5
  × 3

4) 3
  × 4

5) 3
  × 1

6) 3
  × 8

7) 3
  × 6

8) 9
  × 3

9) 3
  × 2

10) 2
   × 3

11) 8
   × 3

12) 4
   × 3

13) 7
   × 3

14) 3
   × 5

15) 6
   × 3

16) 1
   × 3

17) 3
   × 9

18) 1
   × 3

19) 4
   × 3

20) 3
   × 7

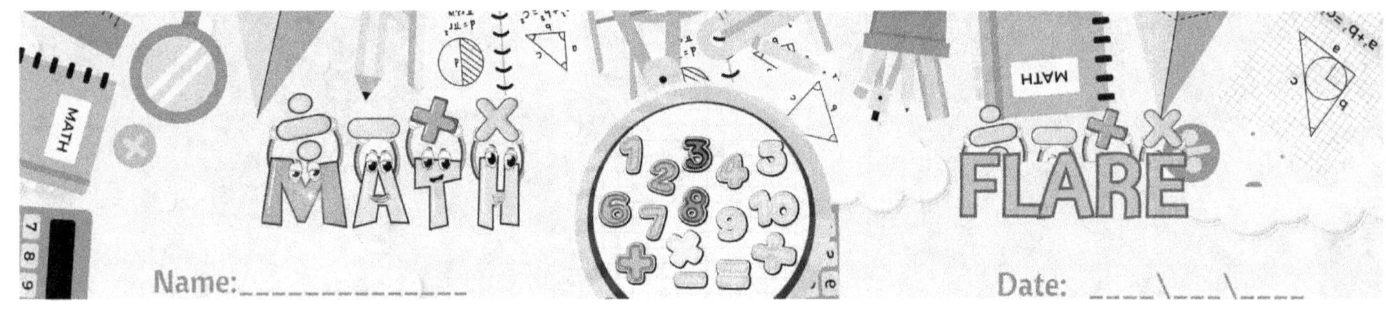

Multiplication by 4

1)   4
   × 8

2)   6
   × 4

3)   7
   × 4

4)   4
   × 2

5)   5
   × 4

6)   4
   × 4

7)   1
   × 4

8)   4
   × 3

9)   4
   × 9

10)   4
   × 6

11)   4
   × 5

12)   3
   × 4

13)   2
   × 4

14)   4
   × 7

15)   8
   × 4

16)   4
   × 1

17)   9
   × 4

18)   8
   × 4

19)   4
   × 2

20)   4
   × 3

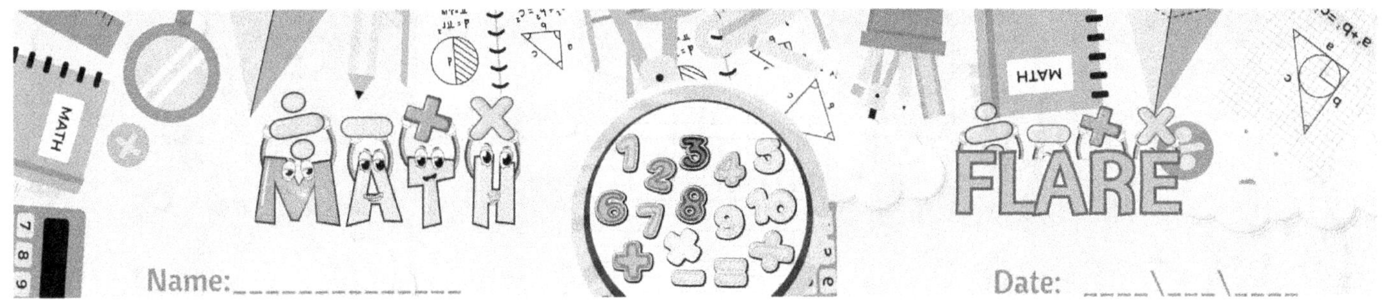

Multiplication by 5

1) 5
   × 4

2) 6
   × 5

3) 5
   × 5

4) 5
   × 2

5) 5
   × 7

6) 3
   × 5

7) 9
   × 5

8) 1
   × 5

9) 5
   × 8

10) 8
    × 5

11) 2
    × 5

12) 4
    × 5

13) 5
    × 9

14) 5
    × 3

15) 5
    × 6

16) 5
    × 1

17) 7
    × 5

18) 5
    × 8

19) 8
    × 5

20) 5
    × 5

MathFlare - Math Workbook 2nd Grade

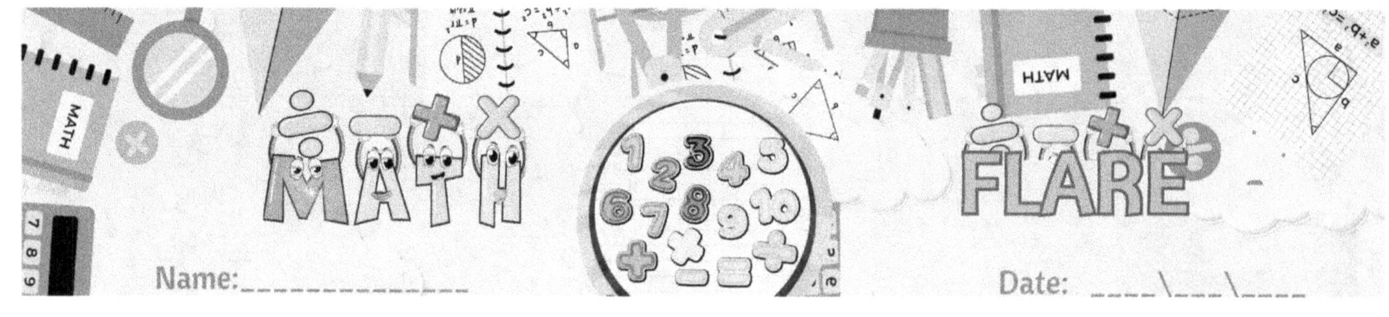

Multiplication by 6

1) 6
  × 6
  ——
  36

2) 6
  × 8
  ——
  48

3) 2
  × 6

4) 6
  × 1

5) 3
  × 6

6) 6
  × 4

7) 6
  × 5

8) 7
  × 6

9) 6
  × 9

10) 9
  × 6

11) 6
  × 2

12) 8
  × 6

13) 4
  × 6

14) 6
  × 7

15) 6
  × 3

16) 5
  × 6

17) 1
  × 6

18) 5
  × 6

19) 6
  × 2

20) 6
  × 3

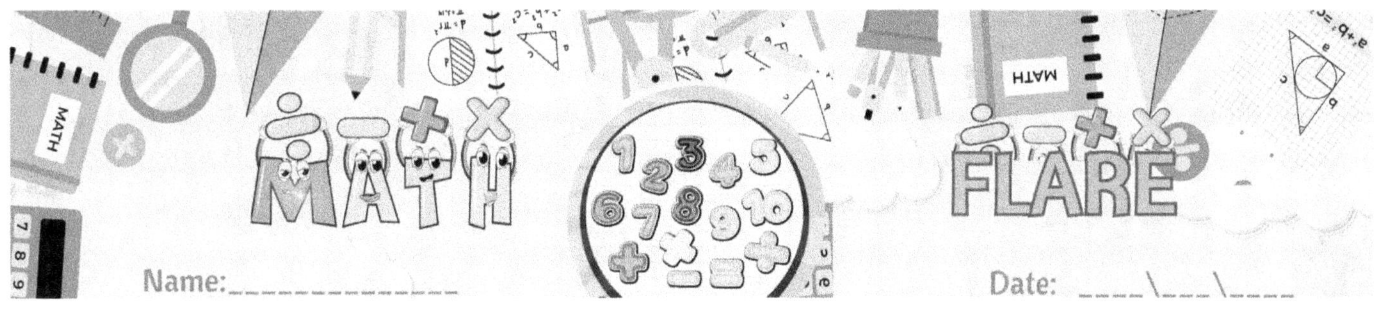

Multiplication by 7

1) 8
   × 7

2) 7
   × 7

3) 7
   × 6

4) 7
   × 2

5) 3
   × 7

6) 7
   × 1

7) 7
   × 5

8) 4
   × 7

9) 9
   × 7

10) 7
    × 8

11) 7
    × 3

12) 6
    × 7

13) 7
    × 4

14) 7
    × 9

15) 2
    × 7

16) 1
    × 7

17) 5
    × 7

18) 7
    × 7

19) 8
    × 7

20) 4
    × 7

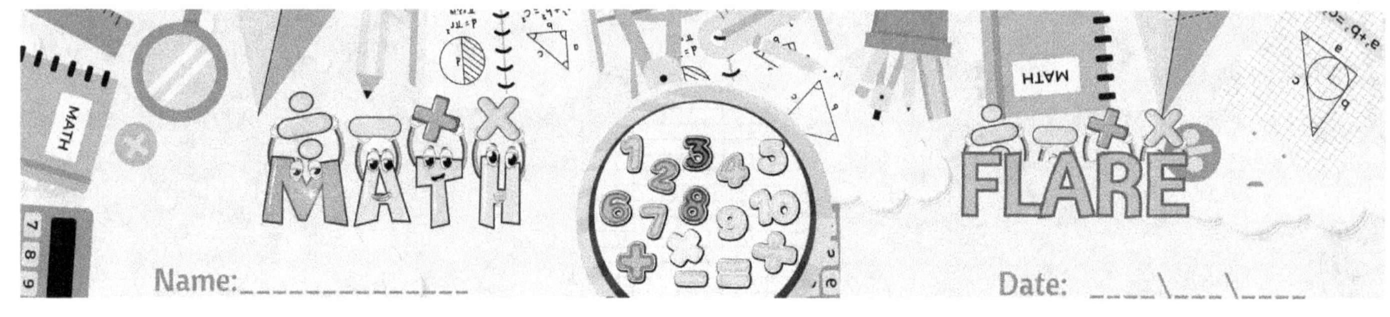

Multiplication by 8

1) 8
  × 2

2) 8
  × 8

3) 8
  × 6

4) 1
  × 8

5) 8
  × 7

6) 4
  × 8

7) 8
  × 5

8) 3
  × 8

9) 9
  × 8

10) 8
  × 4

11) 7
  × 8

12) 5
  × 8

13) 2
  × 8

14) 8
  × 9

15) 8
  × 3

16) 6
  × 8

17) 8
  × 1

18) 2
  × 8

19) 2
  × 8

20) 8
  × 4

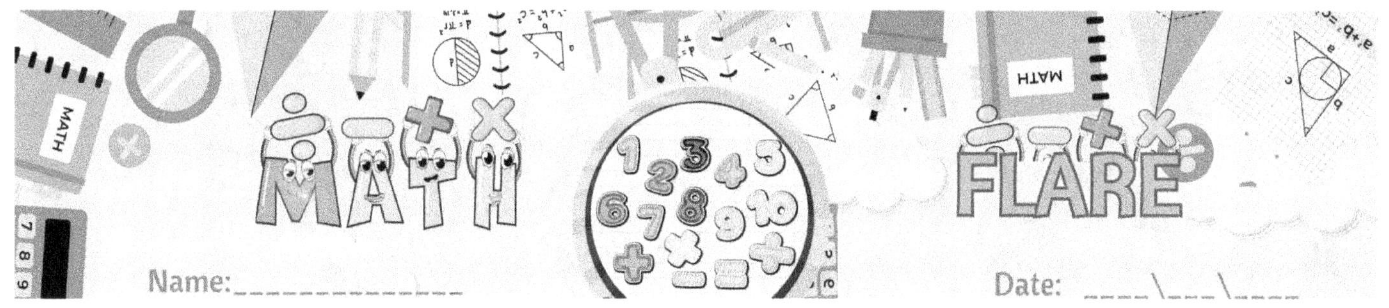

Name:_______________   Date: _______________

Multiplication by 9

1) 3
× 9

27

2) 7
× 9

63

3) 9
× 8
---

4) 2
× 9
---

5) 9
× 4
---

6) 5
× 9
---

7) 6
× 9
---

8) 9
× 9
---

9) 9
× 1
---

10) 9
× 2
---

11) 9
× 6
---

12) 9
× 5
---

13) 8
× 9
---

14) 4
× 9
---

15) 9
× 7
---

16) 9
× 3
---

17) 1
× 9
---

18) 4
× 9
---

19) 3
× 9
---

20) 9
× 5

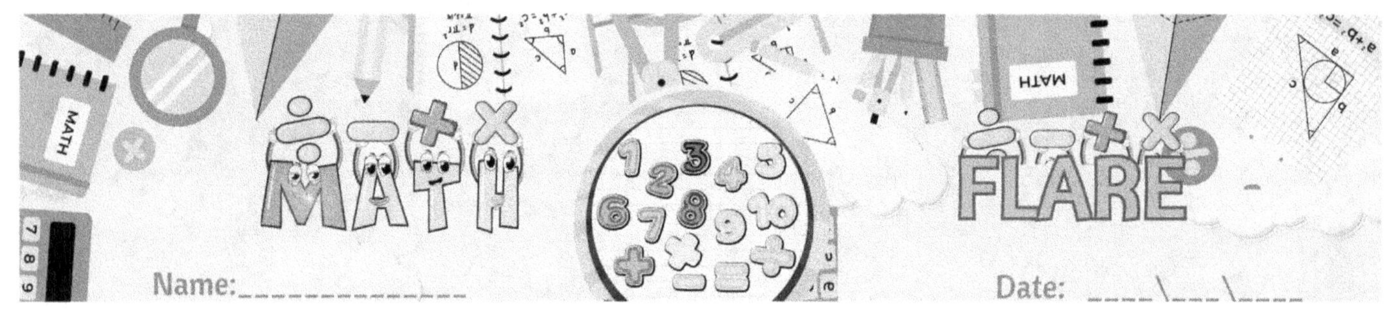

Multiplication by 10

1)   9
  × 10

2)   10
  × 8

3)   6
  × 10

4)   1
  × 10

5)   10
  × 7

6)   10
  × 5

7)   10
  × 3

8)   4
  × 10

9)   2
  × 10

10) 10
  × 2

11) 5
  × 10

12) 10
  × 1

13) 10
  × 6

14) 10
  × 4

15) 8
  × 10

16) 7
  × 10

17) 3
  × 10

18) 10
  × 9

19) 10
  × 4

20) 6
  × 10

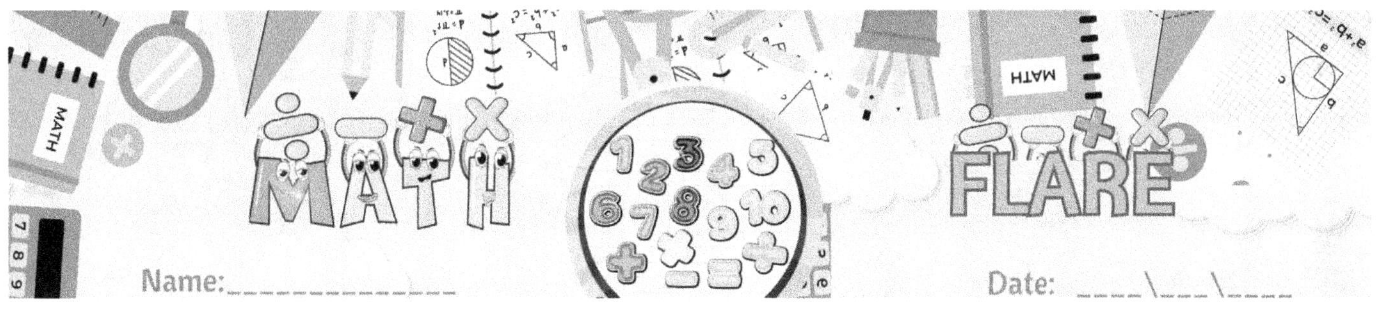

Name:________________ Date: ____________

Basic Multiplication
Find the product.

1) 8
   × 2
   ─────
    16

2) 6
   × 8
   ─────
    48

3) 2
   × 2

4) 1
   × 5

5) 2
   × 3

6) 4
   × 5

7) 10
   × 5

8) 4
   × 7

9) 2
   × 4

10) 8
    × 6

11) 9
    × 3

12) 9
    × 5

13) 9
    × 4

14) 3
    × 7

15) 4
    × 6

16) 4
    × 3

17) 7
    × 9

18) 10
    × 8

19) 2
    × 5

20) 1
    × 6

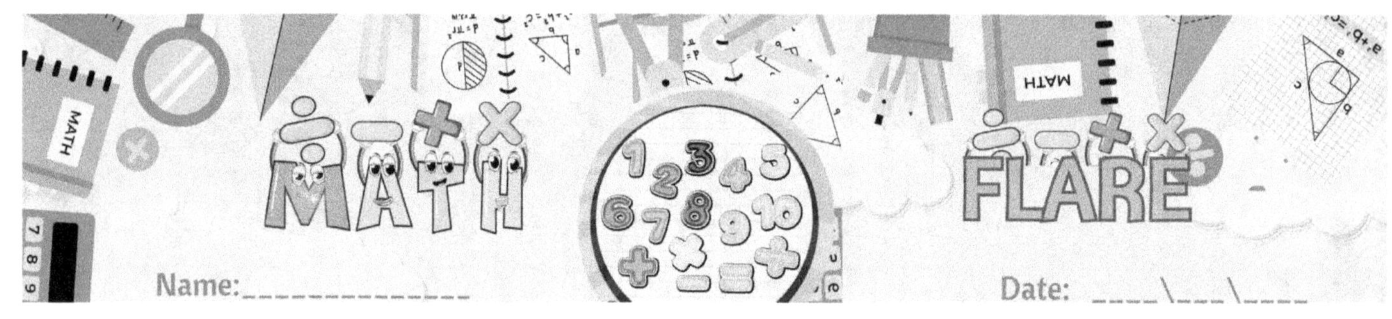

Name:_________________   Date: _______________

21)   10
  × 9

22)   4
  × 8

23)   8
  × 10

24)   4
  × 4

25)   9
  × 7

26)   3
  × 5

27)   5
  × 1

28)   2
  × 8

29)   8
  × 5

30)   8
  × 4

31)   3
  × 4

32)   6
  × 3

33)   3
  × 10

34)   7
  × 8

35)   5
  × 10

36)   7
  × 2

37)   1
  × 4

38)   5
  × 5

39)   3
  × 6

40)   8
  × 9

MathFlare - Math Workbook 2nd Grade

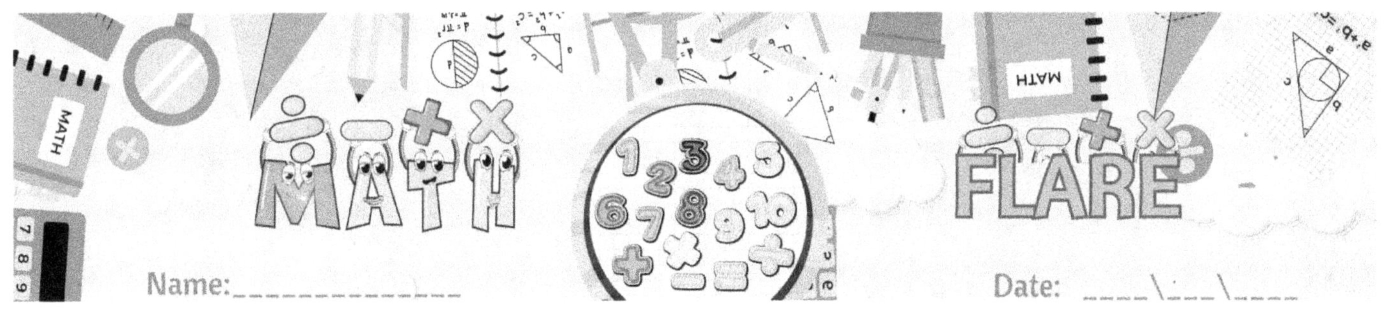

41) $\begin{array}{r} 7 \\ \times\ 1 \\ \hline \end{array}$	42) $\begin{array}{r} 2 \\ \times\ 9 \\ \hline \end{array}$	43) $\begin{array}{r} 8 \\ \times\ 7 \\ \hline \end{array}$	44) $\begin{array}{r} 6 \\ \times\ 2 \\ \hline \end{array}$
45) $\begin{array}{r} 9 \\ \times\ 8 \\ \hline \end{array}$	46) $\begin{array}{r} 1 \\ \times\ 10 \\ \hline \end{array}$	47) $\begin{array}{r} 1 \\ \times\ 3 \\ \hline \end{array}$	48) $\begin{array}{r} 5 \\ \times\ 6 \\ \hline \end{array}$
49) $\begin{array}{r} 1 \\ \times\ 1 \\ \hline \end{array}$	50) $\begin{array}{r} 5 \\ \times\ 9 \\ \hline \end{array}$	51) $\begin{array}{r} 8 \\ \times\ 1 \\ \hline \end{array}$	52) $\begin{array}{r} 5 \\ \times\ 8 \\ \hline \end{array}$
53) $\begin{array}{r} 3 \\ \times\ 2 \\ \hline \end{array}$	54) $\begin{array}{r} 5 \\ \times\ 4 \\ \hline \end{array}$	55) $\begin{array}{r} 5 \\ \times\ 7 \\ \hline \end{array}$	56) $\begin{array}{r} 7 \\ \times\ 5 \\ \hline \end{array}$
57) $\begin{array}{r} 6 \\ \times\ 7 \\ \hline \end{array}$	58) $\begin{array}{r} 1 \\ \times\ 9 \\ \hline \end{array}$	59) $\begin{array}{r} 5 \\ \times\ 2 \\ \hline \end{array}$	60) $\begin{array}{r} 7 \\ \times\ 6 \\ \hline \end{array}$

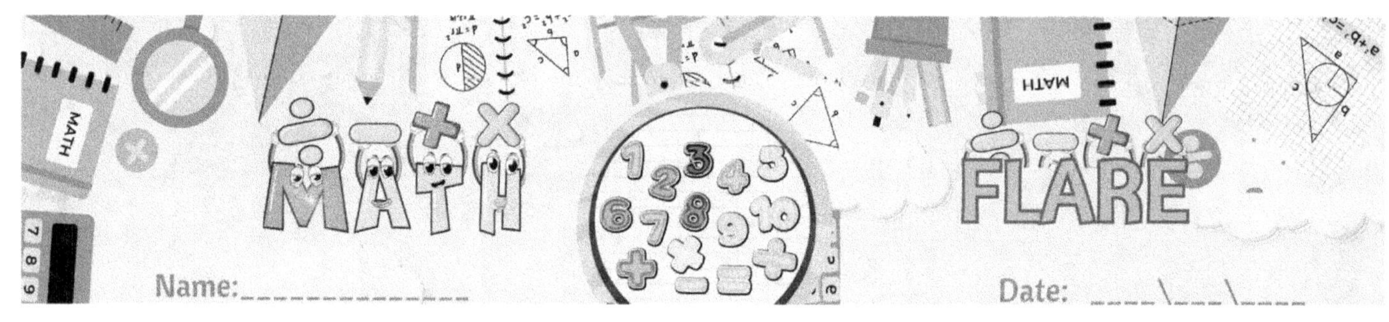

61) 2
× 7

62) 5
× 3

63) 4
× 1

64) 6
× 9

65) 6
× 6

66) 3
× 3

67) 1
× 7

68) 4
× 10

69) 10
×   3

70) 4
× 2

71) 2
× 6

72) 9
× 6

73) 6
× 5

74) 7
× 7

75) 9
× 2

76) 7
× 4

77) 10
×   1

78) 6
× 4

79) 9
× 10

80) 1
× 8

MathFlare - Math Workbook 2nd Grade

103

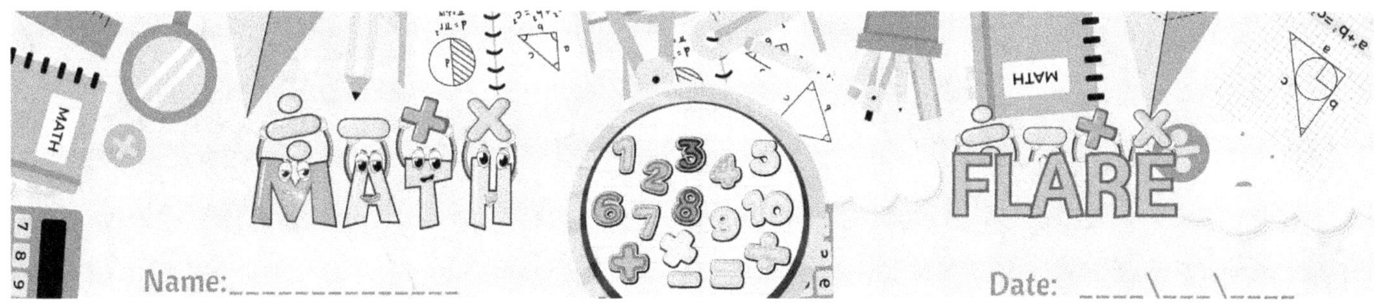

81) 9 × 9	82) 1 × 2	83) 8 × 8	84) 8 × 3
85) 4 × 9	86) 9 × 1	87) 3 × 9	88) 10 × 10
89) 2 × 10	90) 10 × 6	91) 2 × 1	92) 10 × 7
93) 3 × 8	94) 6 × 10	95) 3 × 1	96) 6 × 1
97) 10 × 2	98) 7 × 3	99) 7 × 10	100) 10 × 4

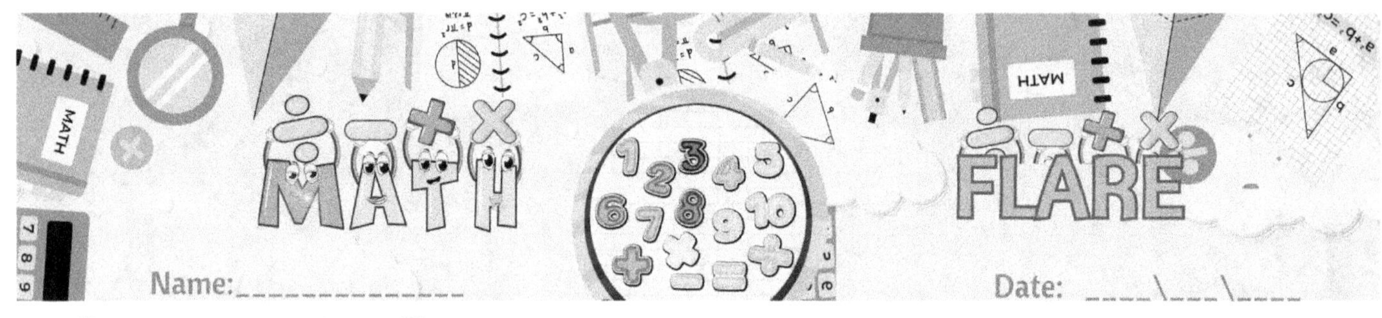

Name:______________________   Date: ______________

Commutative Property

Use the commutative property to fill the missing values.

1) 8 × 2 = 2 × <u>8</u>

2) 7 × 8 = 8 × __

3) 1 × 6 = __ × 1

4) 7 × __ = 5 × 7

5) 4 × __ = 5 × 4

6) 3 × 9 = 9 × __

7) 9 × __ = 5 × 9

8) 3 × 6 = __ × 3

9) 3 × 8 = __ × 3

10) 10 × 5 = __ × 10

11) 3 × 7 = 7 × __

12) 6 × __ = 5 × 6

13) 9 × __ = 2 × 9

14) 5 × __ = 7 × 5

15) 4 × 6 = __ × 4

16) 4 × 7 = __ × 4

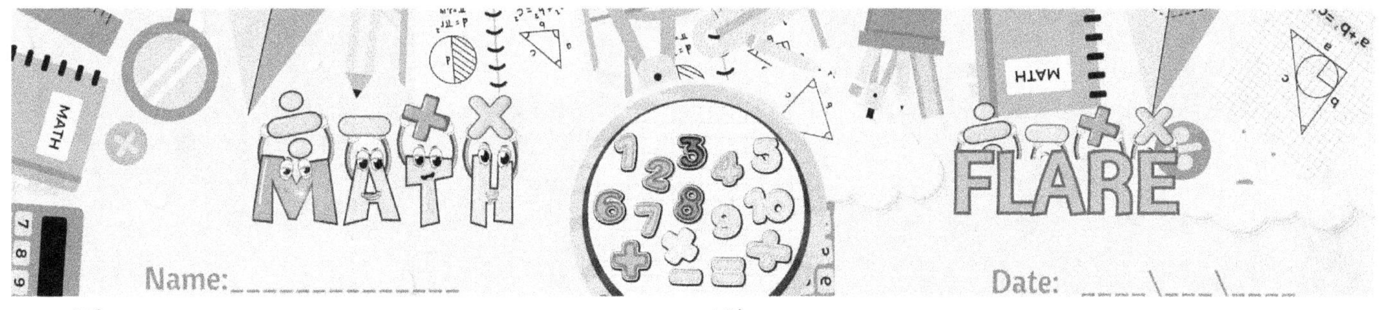

17) 9 × __ = 3 × 9

18) 3 × 10 = __ × 3

19) 6 × 2 = __ × 6

20) 5 × __ = 1 × 5

21) 2 × 7 = 7 × __

22) __ × 9 = 9 × 2

23) 9 × 1 = __ × 9

24) __ × 3 = 3 × 6

25) 5 × 9 = __ × 5

26) 5 × __ = 2 × 5

27) 4 × 9 = __ × 4

28) __ × 4 = 4 × 2

29) 2 × 8 = 8 × __

30) 8 × __ = 5 × 8

31) 5 × __ = 6 × 5

32) 1 × 9 = __ × 1

33) 1 × __ = 7 × 1

34) 7 × __ = 3 × 7

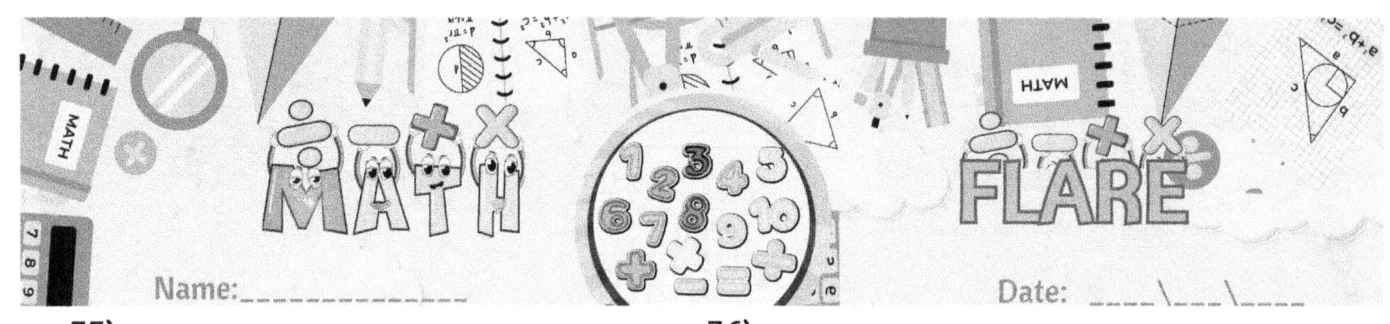

35) __ × 3 = 3 × 1

36) __ × 7 = 7 × 9

37) __ × 5 = 5 × 1

38) 8 × 3 = __ × 8

39) ___ × 9 = 9 × 10

40) __ × 6 = 6 × 8

41) 7 × 1 = __ × 7

42) 1 × 8 = __ × 1

43) 3 × 4 = 4 × __

44) 9 × __ = 6 × 9

45) 3 × 2 = 2 × __

46) 10 × 4 = __ × 10

47) 6 × 9 = 9 × __

48) 8 × 1 = __ × 8

49) __ × 10 = 10 × 5

50) 2 × __ = 5 × 2

51) 7 × 10 = 10 × __

52) 7 × __ = 2 × 7

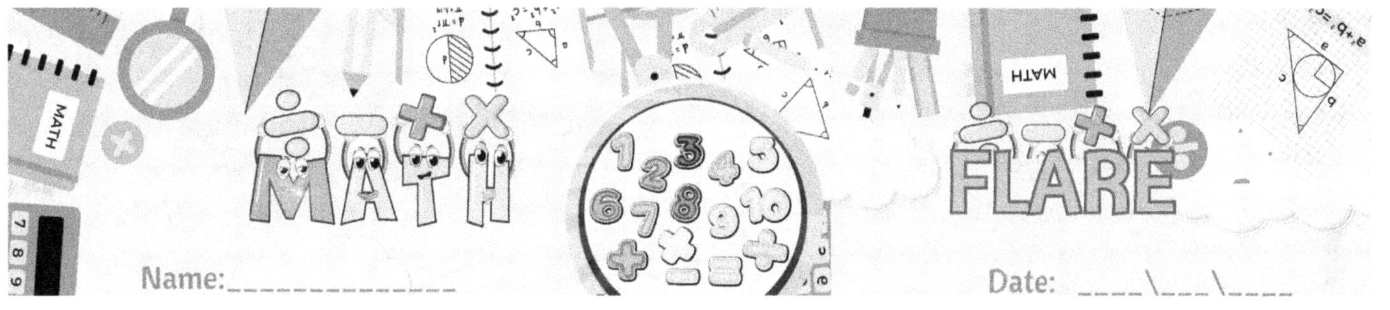

Matching the answers.

1)

a. 19 − 2 = _______   •   • J = 118

b. 80 − 52 = ______   •   • B = 17

c. 47 + 89 = ______   •   • A = 28

d. 26 + 93 = ______   •   • G = 38

e. 86 − 48 = ______   •   • D = 136

f. 5 − 3 = _______   •   • F = 99

g. 73 + 45 = ______   •   • I = 119

h. 43 − 3 = _______   •   • H = 154

i. 54 + 45 = ______   •   • E = 40

j. 87 + 67 = ______   •   • C = 2

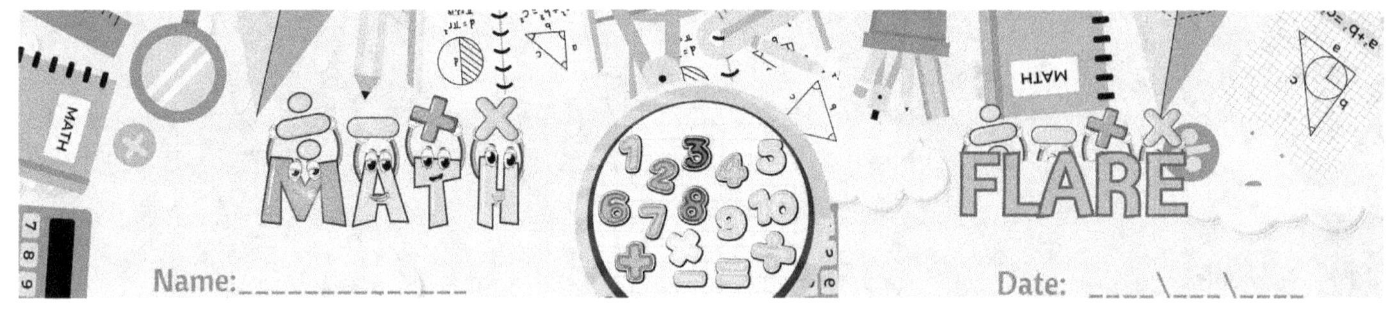

2)

a. 50 + 36 = _______   •   • C = 5

b. 83 + 47 = _______   •   • F = 160

c. 90 + 9 = _______   •   • H = 99

d. 52 - 18 = _______   •   • J = 52

e. 63 + 97 = _______   •   • B = 160

f. 14 - 9 = _______   •   • I = 34

g. 95 + 79 = _______   •   • D = 174

h. 40 + 12 = _______   •   • A = 86

i. 2 + 13 = _______   •   • E = 130

j. 75 + 85 = _______   •   • G = 15

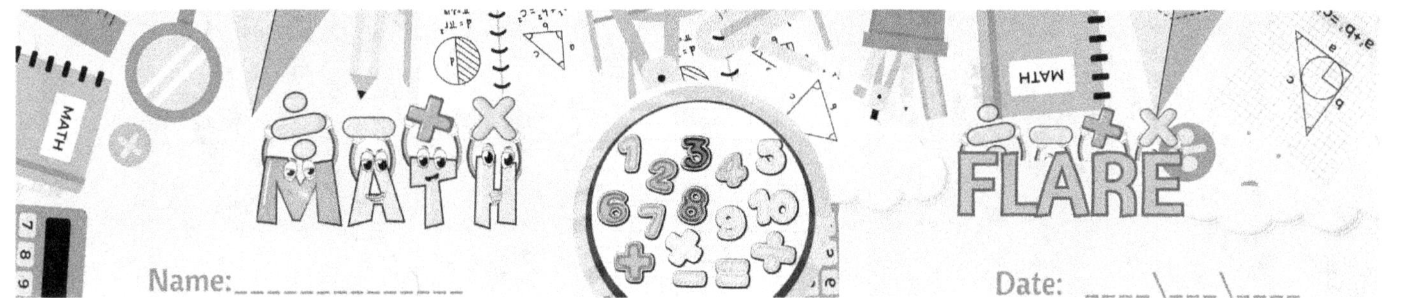

Name:_______________   Date: _______________

3)

a. 27 + 49 = ________   •

b. 44 – 8 = ________   •

c. 17 + 98 = ________   •

d. 5 – 1 = ________   •

e. 100 – 13 = ________   •

f. 29 + 96 = ________   •

g. 95 – 87 = ________   •

h. 28 + 75 = ________   •

i. 26 + 29 = ________   •

j. 37 – 12 = ________   •

• I = 87

• C = 4

• D = 36

• F = 55

• B = 115

• H = 8

• E = 76

• A = 103

• G = 125

• J = 25

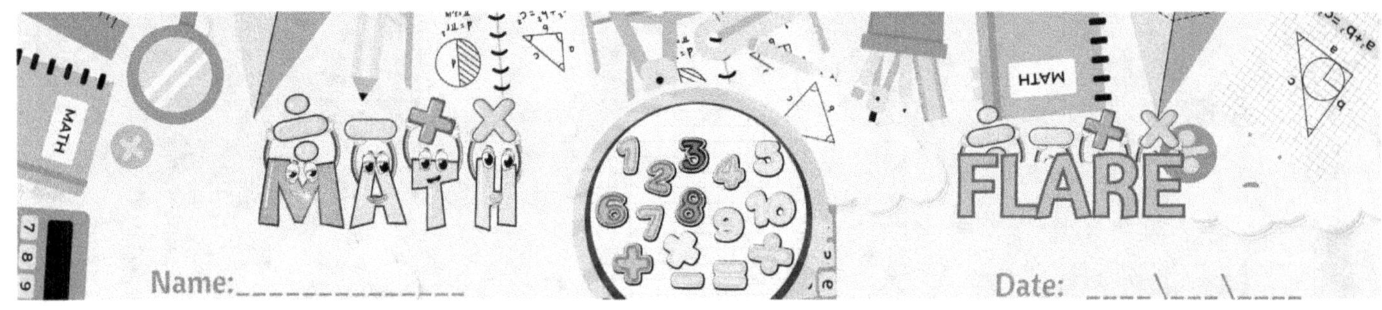

4)

a. 20 + 82 = _______ •	• D = 114
b. 16 - 8 = _______ •	• H = 136
c. 96 + 40 = _______ •	• F = 102
d. 87 + 36 = _______ •	• J = 101
e. 98 + 16 = _______ •	• A = 83
f. 30 - 10 = _______ •	• G = 138
g. 21 + 80 = _______ •	• B = 20
h. 54 + 84 = _______ •	• E = 85
i. 10 + 73 = _______ •	• I = 123
j. 72 + 13 = _______ •	• C = 8

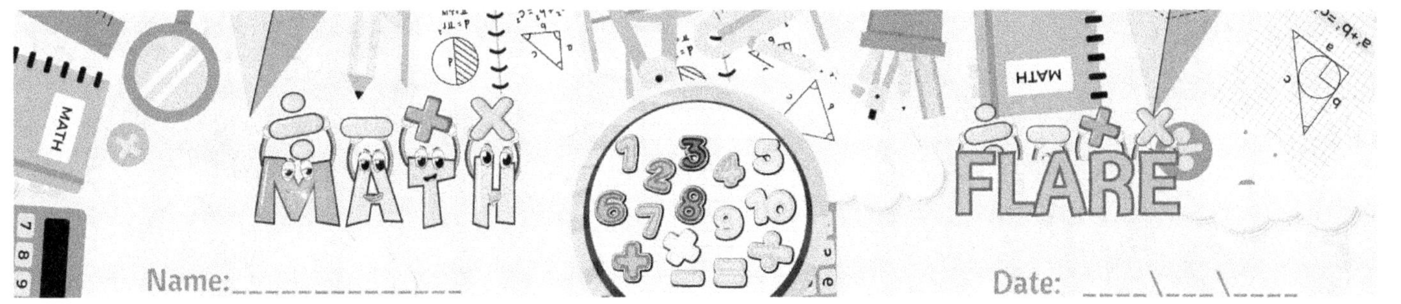

5)

a. 81 + 97 = _______   •

b. 93 – 47 = ______   •

c. 52 – 38 = ______   •

d. 47 – 42 = ______   •

e. 63 + 29 = ______   •

f. 90 + 8 = _______   •

g. 2 – 1 = _______   •

h. 45 + 1 = _______   •

i. 85 + 57 = ______   •

j. 13 + 24 = ______   •

• F = 98

• B = 46

• H = 37

• A = 5

• C = 46

• I = 92

• E = 1

• G = 178

• J = 142

• D = 14

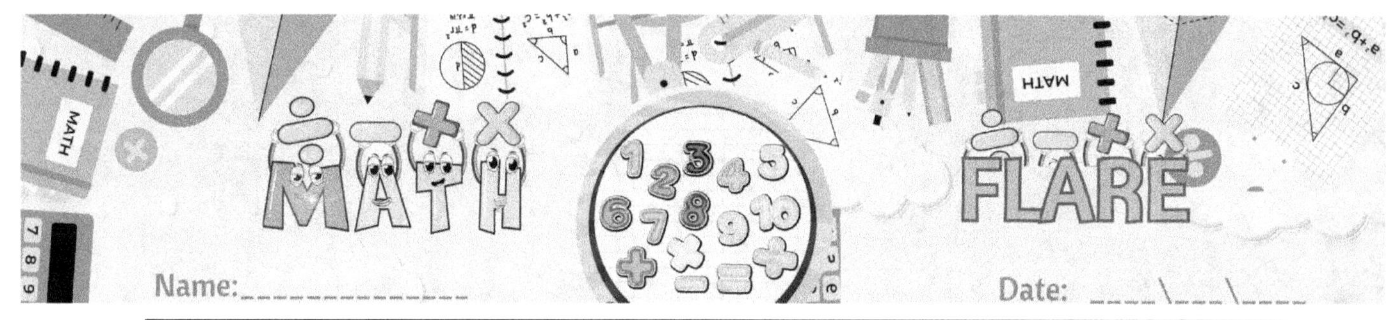

Name:________________   Date: ____________

6)

a. 1 + 6 = __________   •   • J = 68

b. 62 + 6 = ________   •   • C = 105

c. 87 - 78 = ______   •   • I = 5

d. 22 + 83 = ______   •   • G = 128

e. 90 - 76 = ______   •   • A = 9

f. 67 + 47 = ______   •   • H = 114

g. 95 + 83 = ______   •   • F = 7

h. 48 + 80 = ______   •   • E = 35

i. 41 - 6 = ________   •   • D = 14

j. 26 - 21 = ______   •   • B = 178

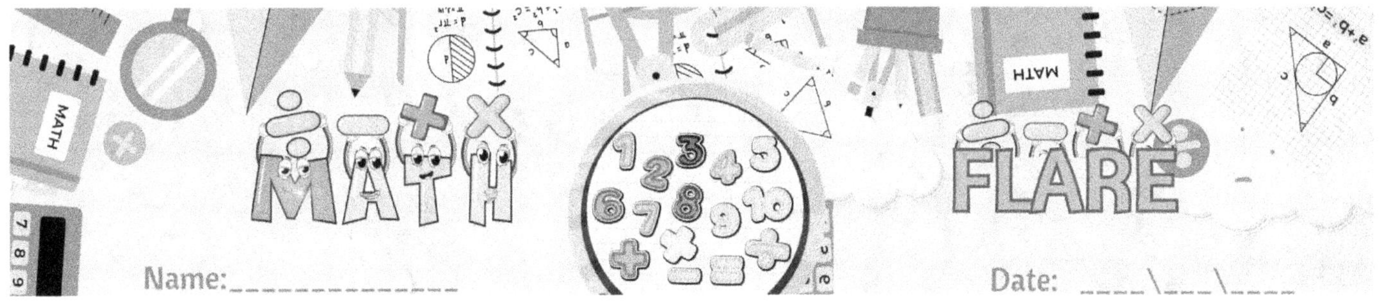

7)

a. 36 – 1 = _______ •

b. 43 + 3 = _______ •

c. 41 + 80 = _______ •

d. 59 + 55 = _______ •

e. 90 + 18 = _______ •

f. 22 + 54 = _______ •

g. 43 + 22 = _______ •

h. 24 – 22 = _______ •

i. 43 + 69 = _______ •

j. 6 – 3 = _______ •

• J = 65

• F = 2

• E = 3

• A = 121

• C = 108

• H = 114

• G = 46

• B = 76

• D = 112

• I = 35

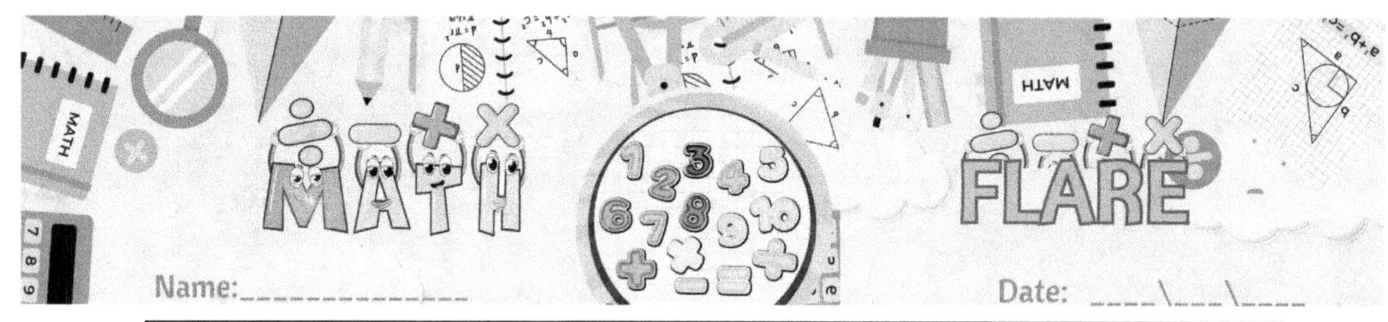

8)

a. 62 + 48 = _______ •   • C = 23

b. 50 + 73 = _______ •   • J = 123

c. 76 - 10 = _______ •   • E = 110

d. 56 - 33 = _______ •   • F = 2

e. 56 - 9 = _______ •   • B = 44

f. 19 - 9 = _______ •   • A = 66

g. 93 - 32 = _______ •   • D = 52

h. 43 - 41 = _______ •   • I = 47

i. 17 + 35 = _______ •   • H = 61

j. 51 - 7 = _______ •   • G = 10

MathFlare - Math Workbook 2nd Grade   **115**

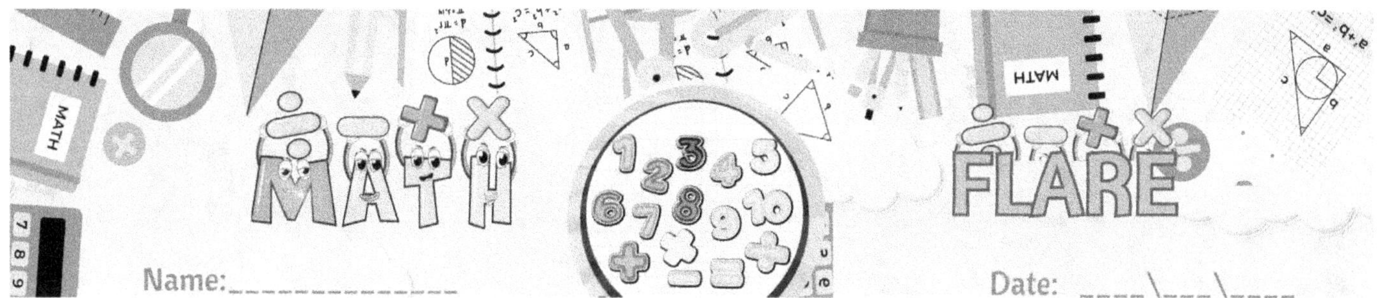

Name:________________ Date: ___________

9)

a. 81 + 15 = _______ •	• B = 94
b. 85 − 42 = _______ •	• D = 139
c. 14 − 10 = _______ •	• F = 1
d. 8 − 7 = _______ •	• H = 96
e. 17 − 16 = _______ •	• G = 164
f. 27 + 53 = _______ •	• I = 74
g. 65 + 99 = _______ •	• E = 1
h. 82 − 8 = _______ •	• A = 4
i. 94 + 45 = _______ •	• J = 80
j. 58 + 36 = _______ •	• C = 43

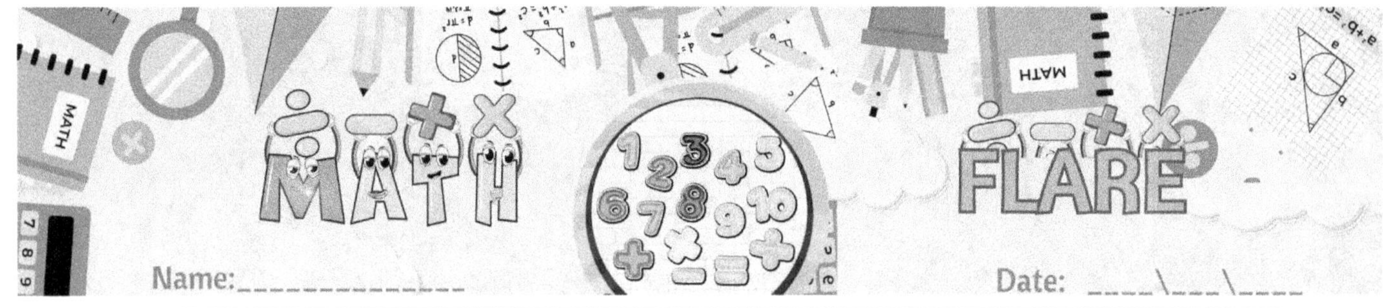

10)

a. 10 - 9 = _______ •	• A = 0
b. 95 - 36 = _______ •	• J = 4
c. 5 - 5 = _______ •	• I = 42
d. 84 + 4 = _______ •	• H = 89
e. 85 + 4 = _______ •	• G = 49
f. 97 - 93 = _______ •	• E = 88
g. 32 + 66 = _______ •	• C = 109
h. 94 + 15 = _______ •	• D = 1
i. 62 - 13 = _______ •	• B = 59
j. 88 - 46 = _______ •	• F = 98

Chapter. 03

Place Value and Expanded Notation

Place value tells us the value of a digit in a number based on where it's placed.

Imagine we have the number 643. It has three digits: 6, 4, and 3.

Now, each digit holds a special place:

- The digit 6 is in the hundreds place. It means it's representing six groups of 100.
- The digit 4 is in the tens place. It means it's representing four groups of 10.
- The digit 3 is in the ones place. It means it's representing three single units.

So, when we want to know the total value of the number 643, we add up the values of each digit based on its place value:

- The digit 6 in the hundreds place is worth 600.
- The digit 4 in the tens place is worth 40.
- The digit 3 in the ones place is worth 3.

When we add these values together, we find the value of the entire number:

$$600 + 40 + 3 = 643$$

Expanded notation helps us see the individual value of each digit in a number and how they contribute to the overall value of the number. It's like breaking down a big puzzle into smaller pieces to understand it better!

So, in expanded notation, we can write 643 as: 600 (from the hundreds place) + 40 (from the tens place) + 3 (from the ones place).

Let's solve problems from the exercises:

Place value of the underlined digit:

$$10\underline{1} = \underline{\quad 1 \text{ one} \quad}$$

Expanded Notations

$$\underline{\quad 26 \quad} \quad 2 \text{ tens} + 6 \text{ ones}$$

$$418 \quad \underline{4 \text{ hundreds} + 1 \text{ ten}}$$
$$\underline{+ \ 8 \text{ ones}}$$

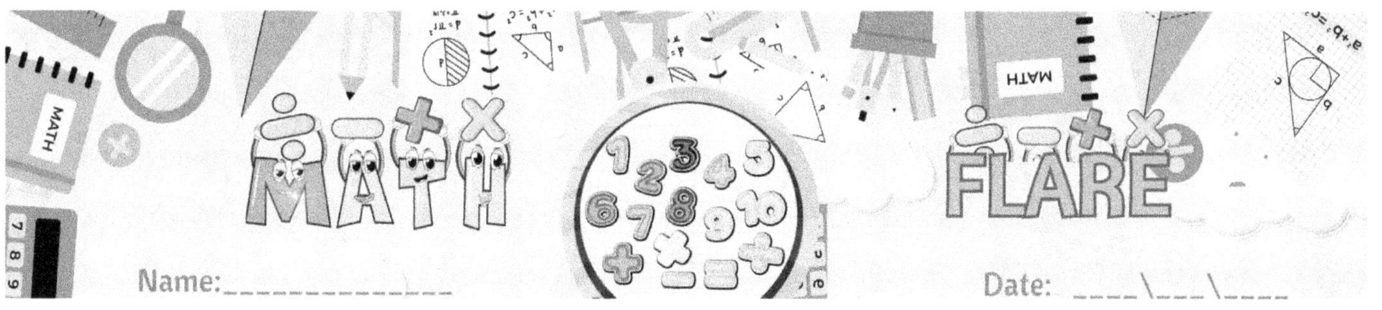

Name:______________   Date: ____________

Place Value

Determine the place value of the underlined digit.

1) 10<u>1</u> = ___1 one___

2) <u>9</u>71 = ___9 hundreds___

3) <u>3</u>02 = _______________

4) 6<u>8</u>0 = _______________

5) 8<u>4</u>3 = _______________

6) 3<u>5</u>8 = _______________

7) 2<u>8</u>0 = _______________

8) <u>5</u>90 = _______________

9) <u>7</u>10 = _______________

10) 71<u>3</u> = _______________

11) 2<u>0</u>8 = _______________

12) 1<u>2</u>2 = _______________

13) <u>3</u>68 = _______________

14) 33<u>4</u> = _______________

15) <u>7</u>92 = _______________

16) 54<u>7</u> = _______________

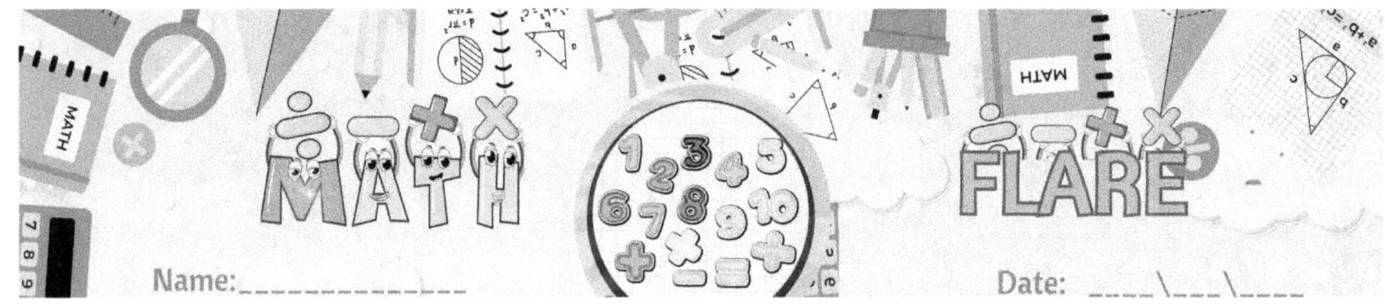

17) 251 = _________________

18) 888 = _________________

19) 719 = _________________

20) 565 = _________________

21) 576 = _________________

22) 347 = _________________

23) 788 = _________________

24) 875 = _________________

25) 273 = _________________

26) 493 = _________________

27) 771 = _________________

28) 435 = _________________

29) 306 = _________________

30) 6 = _________________

31) 923 = _________________

32) 910 = _________________

33) 959 = _________________

34) 502 = _________________

35) 397 = _______________

36) 858 = _______________

37) 392 = _______________

38) 372 = _______________

39) 223 = _______________

40) 556 = _______________

41) 722 = _______________

42) 575 = _______________

43) 291 = _______________

44) 458 = _______________

45) 628 = _______________

46) 456 = _______________

47) 789 = _______________

48) 802 = _______________

49) 869 = _______________

50) 850 = _______________

51) 982 = _______________

52) 27 = _______________

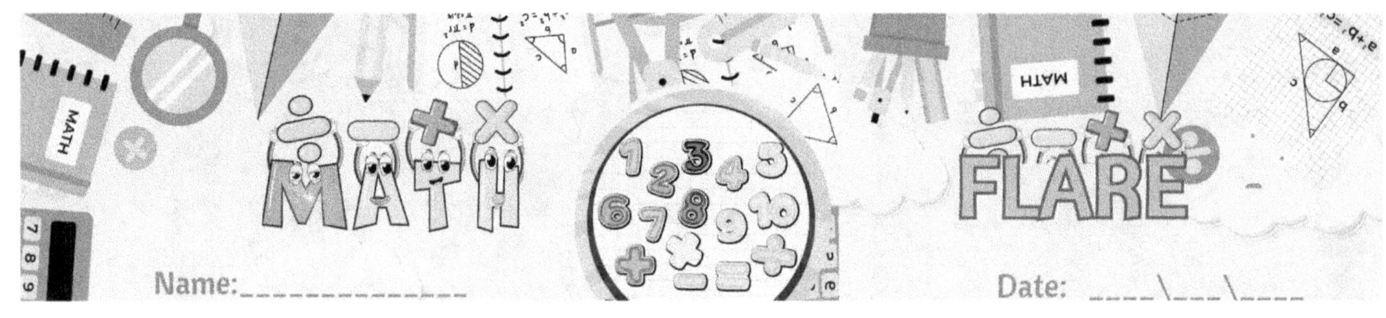

53) $\underline{3}10$ = _______________

54) $3\underline{8}4$ = _______________

55) $7\underline{5}4$ = _______________

56) $18\underline{4}$ = _______________

57) $\underline{4}27$ = _______________

58) $40\underline{8}$ = _______________

59) $3\underline{5}1$ = _______________

60) $5\underline{8}7$ = _______________

61) $3\underline{0}$ = _______________

62) $15\underline{6}$ = _______________

63) $4\underline{0}5$ = _______________

64) $70\underline{8}$ = _______________

65) $2\underline{8}4$ = _______________

66) $21\underline{2}$ = _______________

67) $4\underline{0}9$ = _______________

68) $83\underline{2}$ = _______________

69) $3\underline{9}6$ = _______________

70) $6\underline{9}0$ = _______________

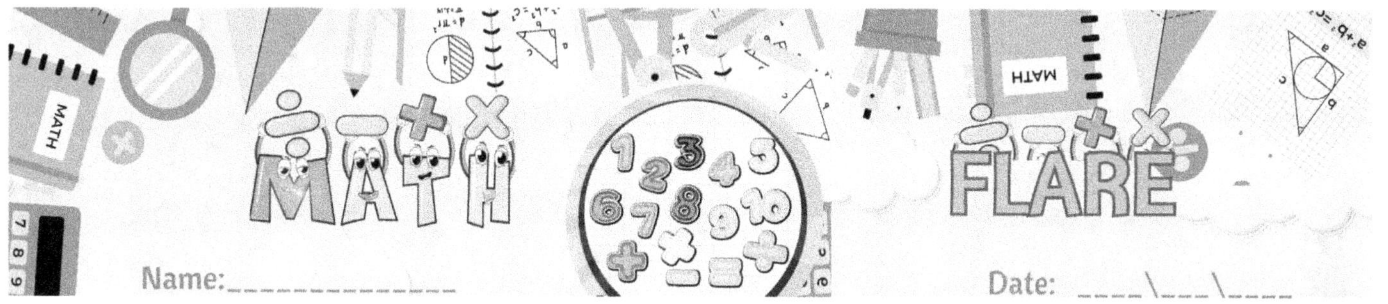

71) 859 = _______________

72) 517 = _______________

73) 497 = _______________

74) 9 = _______________

75) 854 = _______________

76) 498 = _______________

77) 418 = _______________

78) 645 = _______________

79) 38 = _______________

80) 449 = _______________

81) 457 = _______________

82) 24 = _______________

83) 897 = _______________

84) 601 = _______________

85) 748 = _______________

86) 214 = _______________

87) 432 = _______________

88) 984 = _______________

89) 2̲2 = _______________

90) 63̲6 = _______________

91) 52̲7 = _______________

92) 567̲ = _______________

93) 172̲ = _______________

94) 5̲83 = _______________

95) 17̲5 = _______________

96) 4̲16 = _______________

97) 48̲ = _______________

98) 957̲ = _______________

99) 407̲ = _______________

100) 18̲0 = _______________

101) 9̲91 = _______________

102) 46̲6 = _______________

103) 53̲0 = _______________

104) 98̲3 = _______________

105) 6̲86 = _______________

106) 76̲3 = _______________

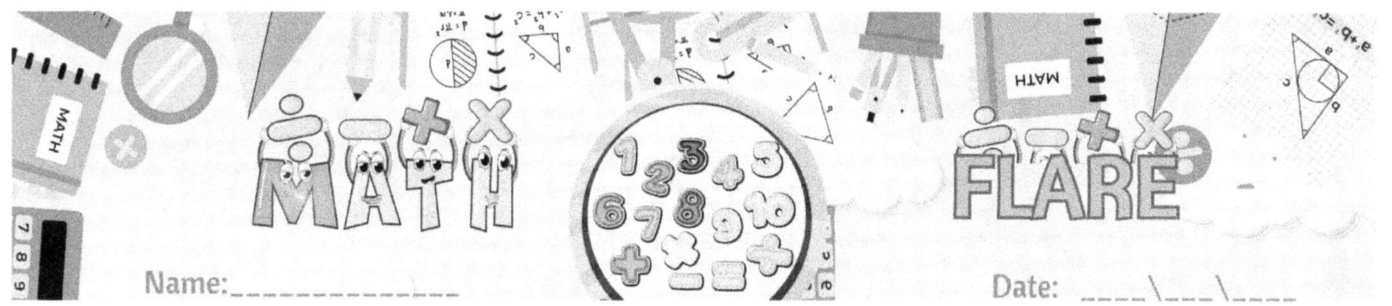

107) 3<u>1</u>4 = _______________

108) <u>6</u>04 = _______________

109) 58<u>1</u> = _______________

110) 94<u>8</u> = _______________

111) 6<u>8</u>5 = _______________

112) 3<u>8</u>7 = _______________

113) <u>6</u>11 = _______________

114) 8<u>3</u>3 = _______________

115) 8<u>5</u> = _______________

116) 1<u>8</u>3 = _______________

117) 259<u>9</u> = _______________

118) <u>4</u>96 = _______________

119) 86<u>1</u> = _______________

120) 4<u>8</u>2 = _______________

121) <u>2</u>88 = _______________

122) 9<u>1</u>5 = _______________

123) 2<u>4</u>4 = _______________

124) 23<u>0</u> = _______________

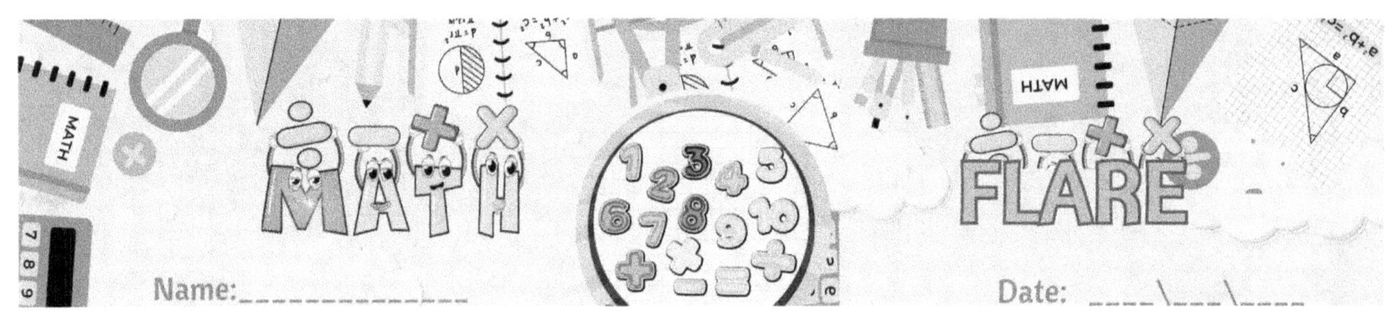

Place Value: Expanded Notation

Provide the expanded notation for each value.

1) __26__ 2 tens + 6 ones

2) ________ 6 hundreds + 8 tens + 9 ones

3) ________ 3 tens + 3 ones

4) ________ 6 hundreds + 7 ones

5) ________ 2 hundreds + 3 tens + 1 one

6) ________ 4 hundreds + 4 tens + 8 ones

7) ________ 6 hundreds + 6 tens + 3 ones

8) ________ 4 hundreds + 4 tens + 4 ones

9) ________ 6 hundreds + 1 ten + 7 ones

10) ________ 6 hundreds + 6 tens + 9 ones

11) ________ 9 hundreds + 8 ones

12) ________ 5 hundreds

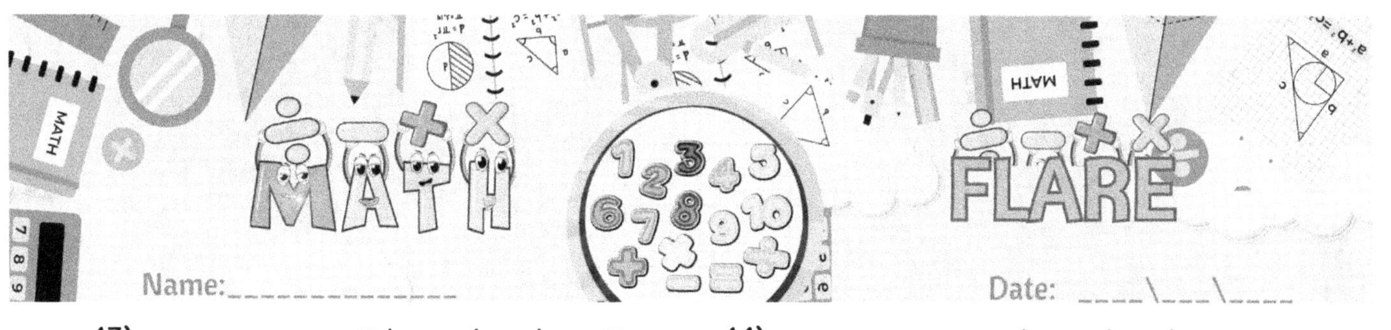

13) __________ 7 hundreds + 7 tens + 9 ones

14) __________ 4 hundreds + 6 tens + 4 ones

15) __________ 1 hundred + 5 tens + 9 ones

16) __________ 3 hundreds + 9 tens + 2 ones

17) __________ 3 hundreds + 6 tens + 8 ones

18) __________ 5 hundreds + 1 ten

19) __________ 6 hundreds + 2 tens + 2 ones

20) __________ 1 hundred + 8 tens

21) __________ 1 hundred + 9 tens + 6 ones

22) __________ 8 hundreds + 3 tens

23) __________ 4 hundreds + 7 tens + 1 one

24) __________ 3 hundreds + 6 tens + 2 ones

25) __________ 2 hundreds + 4 tens + 8 ones

26) __________ 1 hundred + 3 tens + 7 ones

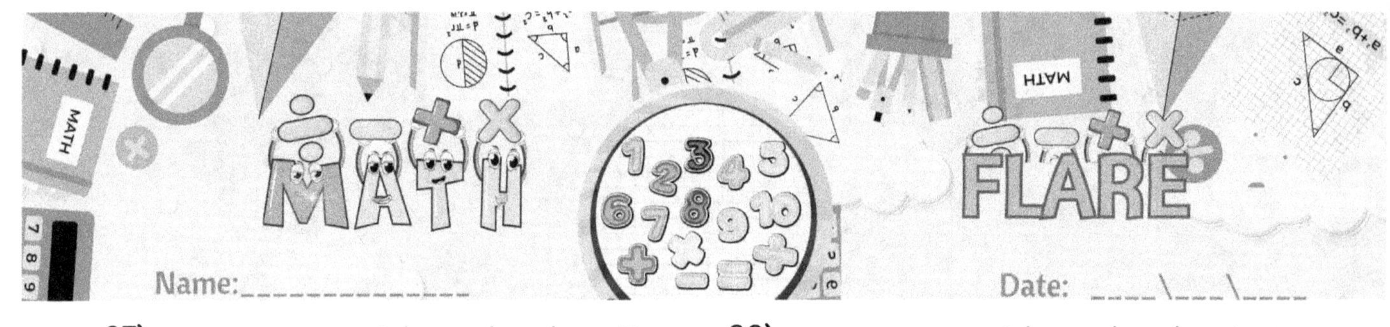

27) __________ 6 hundreds + 3 tens + 5 ones

28) __________ 1 hundred + 1 ten + 1 one

29) __________ 5 hundreds + 6 tens

30) __________ 8 hundreds + 9 tens + 9 ones

31) __________ 8 hundreds + 2 tens + 9 ones

32) __________ 3 hundreds + 8 tens + 6 ones

33) __________ 5 hundreds + 6 tens + 4 ones

34) __________ 3 hundreds + 5 tens + 2 ones

35) __________ 4 hundreds + 3 tens + 8 ones

36) __________ 5 hundreds + 8 ones

37) __________ 3 tens + 2 ones

38) __________ 1 ten + 6 ones

39) __________ 2 hundreds + 4 tens + 1 one

40) __________ 2 hundreds + 6 tens + 8 ones

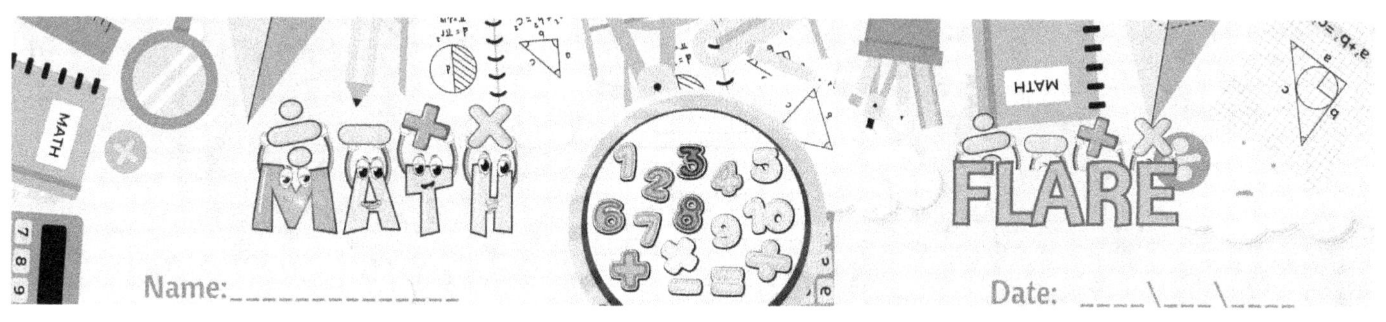

41) __________ 9 hundreds + 7 ones

42) __________ 9 hundreds + 8 tens + 1 one

43) __________ 5 hundreds + 8 tens

44) __________ 3 hundreds + 8 tens + 7 ones

45) __________ 6 hundreds + 2 tens + 6 ones

46) __________ 3 hundreds + 9 tens + 5 ones

47) __________ 3 tens + 9 ones

48) __________ 4 hundreds + 8 tens + 2 ones

49) __________ 1 ten + 1 one

50) __________ 4 hundreds + 9 tens + 2 ones

51) __________ 7 hundreds + 2 tens + 8 ones

52) __________ 4 hundreds

53) __________ 6 hundreds + 4 tens + 4 ones

54) __________ 2 hundreds + 1 ten + 9 ones

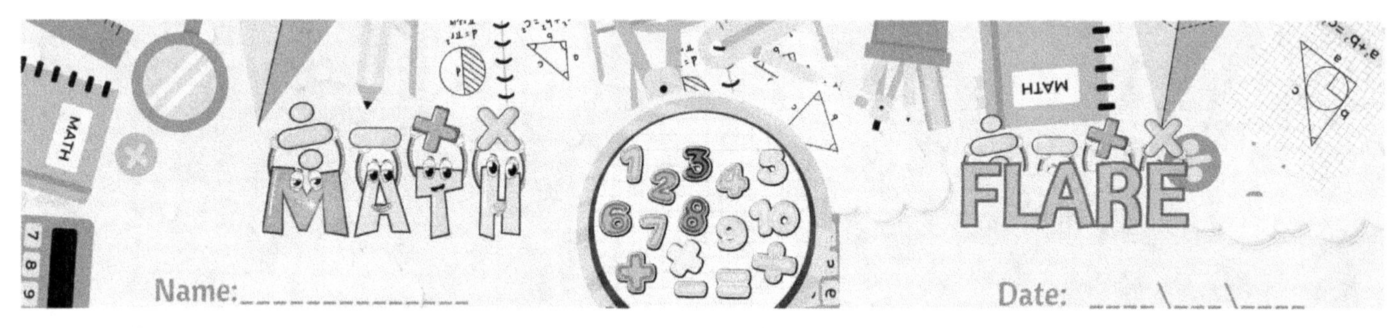

55) __________ 6 hundreds + 7 tens + 1 one

56) __________ 3 hundreds + 6 tens

57) __________ 9 tens + 6 ones

58) __________ 9 hundreds + 8 tens + 4 ones

59) __________ 2 tens + 9 ones

60) __________ 3 hundreds + 3 tens + 5 ones

61) __________ 5 tens + 8 ones

62) __________ 7 hundreds + 7 tens

63) __________ 8 tens + 1 one

64) __________ 1 hundred + 1 ten + 5 ones

65) __________ 2 hundreds + 1 ten + 6 ones

66) __________ 1 hundred + 1 ten + 3 ones

67) __________ 7 hundreds + 2 tens

68) __________ 8 hundreds + 8 tens + 5 ones

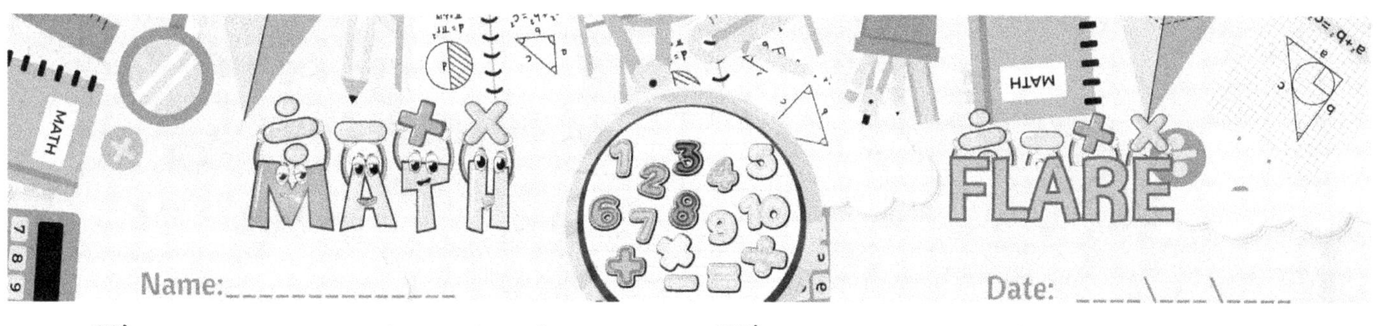

69) __________ 3 hundreds + 3 tens + 7 ones

70) __________ 4 hundreds + 9 tens + 5 ones

71) __________ 3 hundreds + 8 tens + 2 ones

72) __________ 9 hundreds + 1 ten + 2 ones

73) __________ 2 hundreds + 9 tens

74) __________ 8 hundreds + 4 tens + 9 ones

75) __________ 8 hundreds + 9 tens + 1 one

76) __________ 8 hundreds + 6 tens + 1 one

77) __________ 7 tens

78) __________ 5 hundreds + 9 tens + 7 ones

79) __________ 6 hundreds + 2 tens + 8 ones

80) __________ 5 hundreds + 5 tens + 1 one

81) __________ 4 hundreds + 8 ones

82) __________ 1 hundred + 2 ones

83) __________ 9 hundreds + 8 tens + 5 ones

84) __________ 9 hundreds + 2 tens

85) __________ 1 hundred + 5 tens + 8 ones

86) __________ 2 hundreds + 2 tens + 1 one

87) __________ 8 hundreds + 3 tens + 7 ones

88) __________ 6 hundreds + 7 tens + 2 ones

89) __________ 2 hundreds + 5 tens + 7 ones

90) __________ 2 hundreds + 4 tens

91) __________ 5 hundreds + 7 tens + 3 ones

92) __________ 9 hundreds + 2 tens + 4 ones

93) __________ 8 hundreds + 1 ten

94) __________ 2 hundreds + 7 tens + 3 ones

95) __________ 4 hundreds + 1 ten + 2 ones

96) __________ 2 hundreds + 8 tens + 3 ones

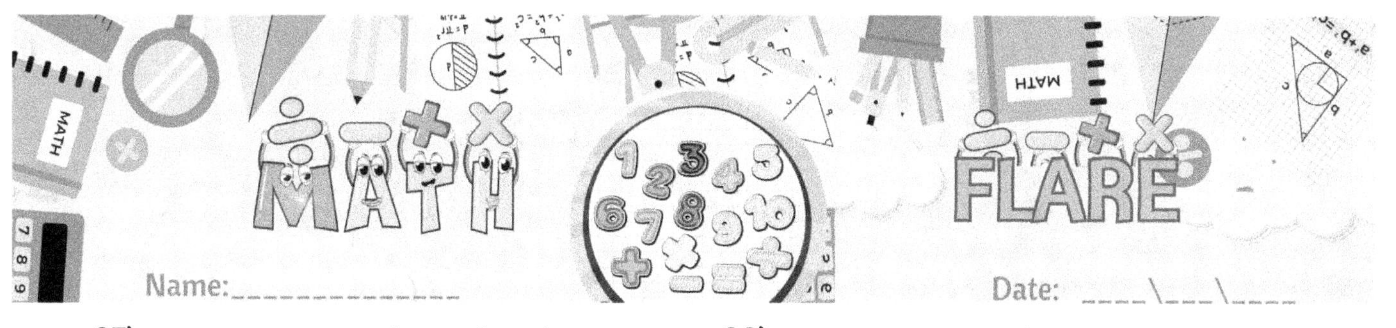

97) __________ 3 hundreds + 1 ten + 9 ones

98) __________ 5 hundreds + 9 tens + 8 ones

99) __________ 6 hundreds + 7 tens + 4 ones

100) __________ 9 hundreds + 9 tens + 6 ones

101) __________ 3 hundreds + 4 tens + 7 ones

102) __________ 4 hundreds + 8 tens + 8 ones

103) __________ 3 hundreds + 5 tens + 5 ones

104) __________ 3 hundreds + 4 tens + 6 ones

105) __________ 3 hundreds + 2 tens + 8 ones

106) __________ 7 hundreds + 8 tens

107) __________ 4 hundreds + 9 tens + 9 ones

108) __________ 5 hundreds + 8 tens + 6 ones

109) __________ 9 hundreds + 1 ten + 5 ones

110) __________ 4 hundreds + 3 tens + 3 ones

 132

111) __________ 7 hundreds + 6 ones

112) __________ 5 hundreds + 7 ones

113) __________ 3 hundreds + 6 tens + 3 ones

114) __________ 9 hundreds + 7 tens + 9 ones

115) __________ 1 hundred + 3 tens

116) __________ 2 hundreds + 9 tens + 5 ones

117) __________ 9 hundreds + 5 tens + 5 ones

118) __________ 4 tens + 9 ones

119) __________ 6 hundreds + 6 tens + 5 ones

120) __________ 5 hundreds + 7 tens + 6 ones

121) __________ 1 hundred + 2 tens + 7 ones

122) __________ 7 hundreds + 1 ten + 7 ones

123) __________ 9 hundreds + 2 tens + 5 ones

124) __________ 8 tens + 2 ones

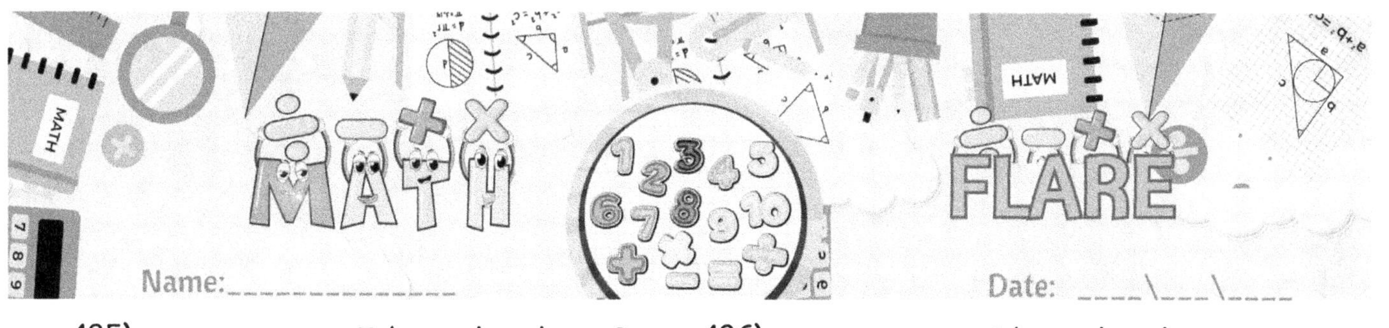

125) __________ 5 hundreds + 9 tens

126) __________ 1 hundred

127) __________ 7 hundreds + 8 tens + 7 ones

128) __________ 2 hundreds + 7 tens + 8 ones

129) __________ 8 hundreds + 7 tens + 7 ones

130) __________ 7 hundreds + 5 tens + 5 ones

131) __________ 4 hundreds + 9 tens + 8 ones

132) __________ 5 hundreds + 6 tens + 6 ones

133) __________ 8 hundreds + 1 ten + 1 one

134) __________ 8 hundreds + 9 tens + 3 ones

135) __________ 1 hundred + 7 tens + 4 ones

136) __________ 3 hundreds + 4 tens + 1 one

137) __________ 8 hundreds + 7 ones

138) __________ 8 hundreds + 6 tens + 7 ones

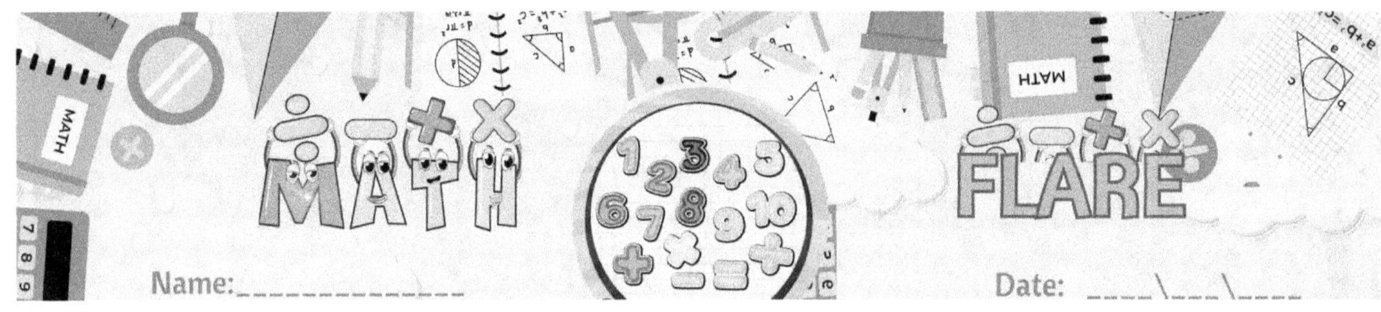

Place Value: Expanded Notation

Provide the expanded notation for each value.

1) 418   4 hundreds + 1 ten + 8 ones

2) 448 _______________

3) 413 _______________

4) 143 _______________

5) 117 _______________

6) 328 _______________

7) 819 _______________

8) 550 _______________

9) 9 _______________

10) 422 _______________

11) 221 _______________

12) 814 _______________

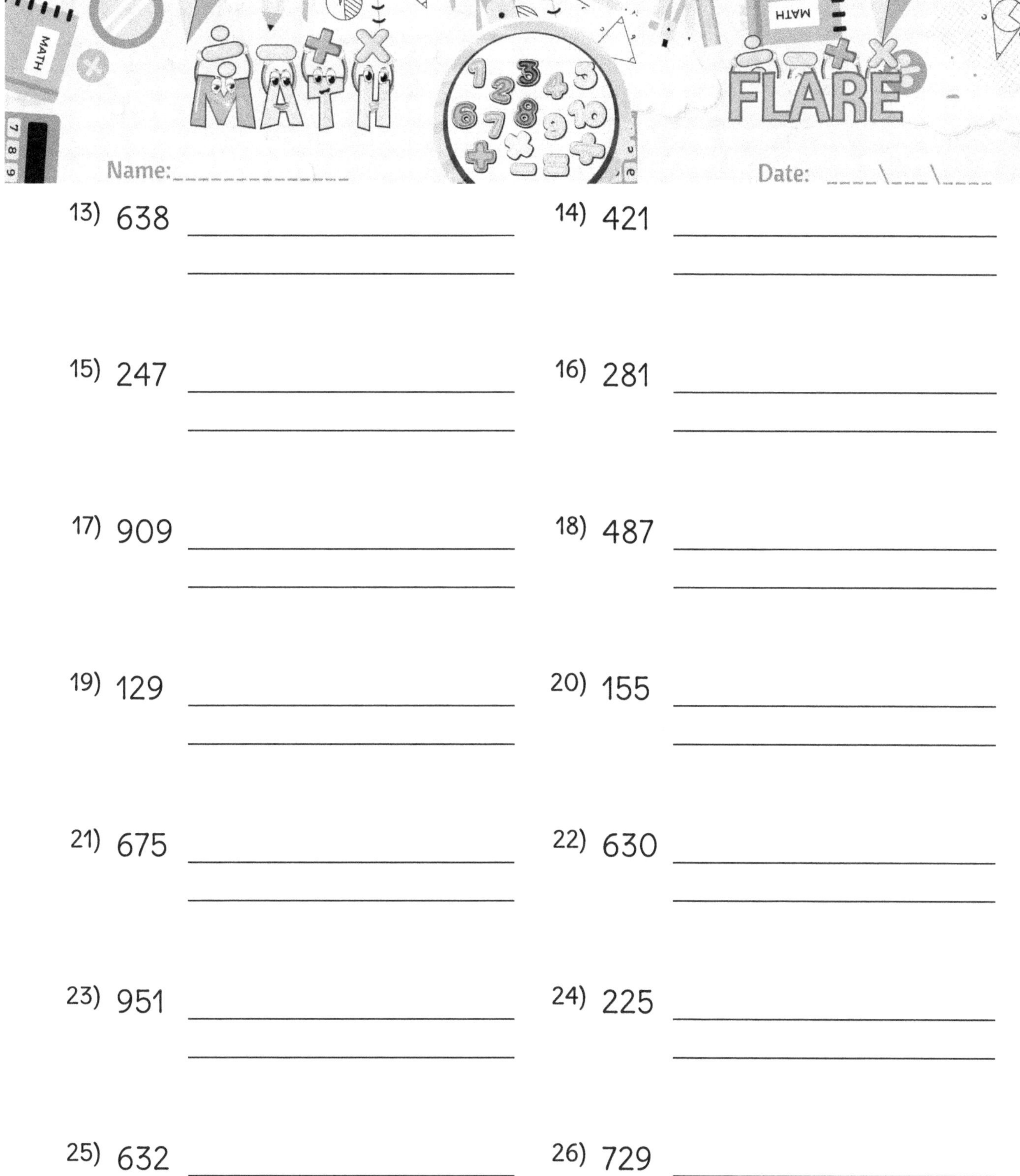

13) 638 __________________

14) 421 __________________

15) 247 __________________

16) 281 __________________

17) 909 __________________

18) 487 __________________

19) 129 __________________

20) 155 __________________

21) 675 __________________

22) 630 __________________

23) 951 __________________

24) 225 __________________

25) 632 __________________

26) 729 __________________

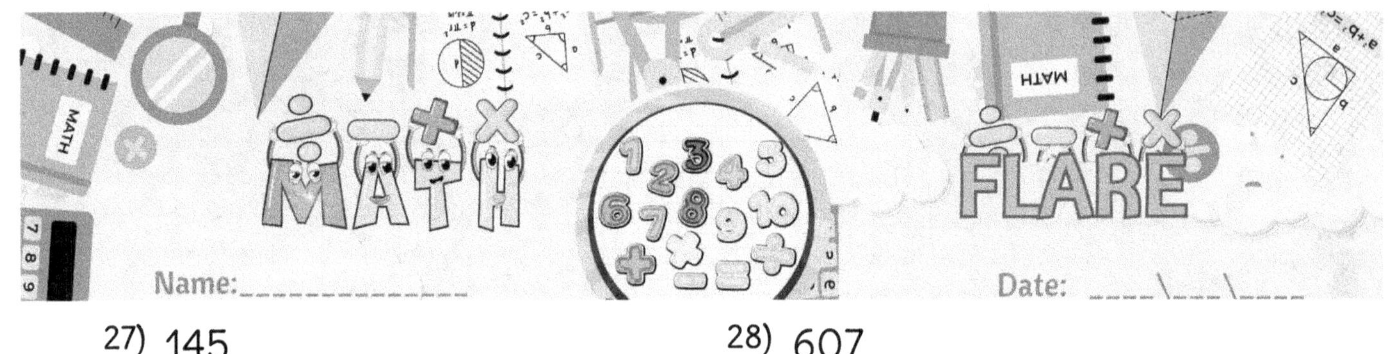

27) 145 _______________________

28) 607 _______________________

29) 990 _______________________

30) 492 _______________________

31) 241 _______________________

32) 785 _______________________

33) 867 _______________________

34) 850 _______________________

35) 508 _______________________

36) 634 _______________________

37) 88 _______________________

38) 447 _______________________

39) 982 _______________________

40) 459 _______________________

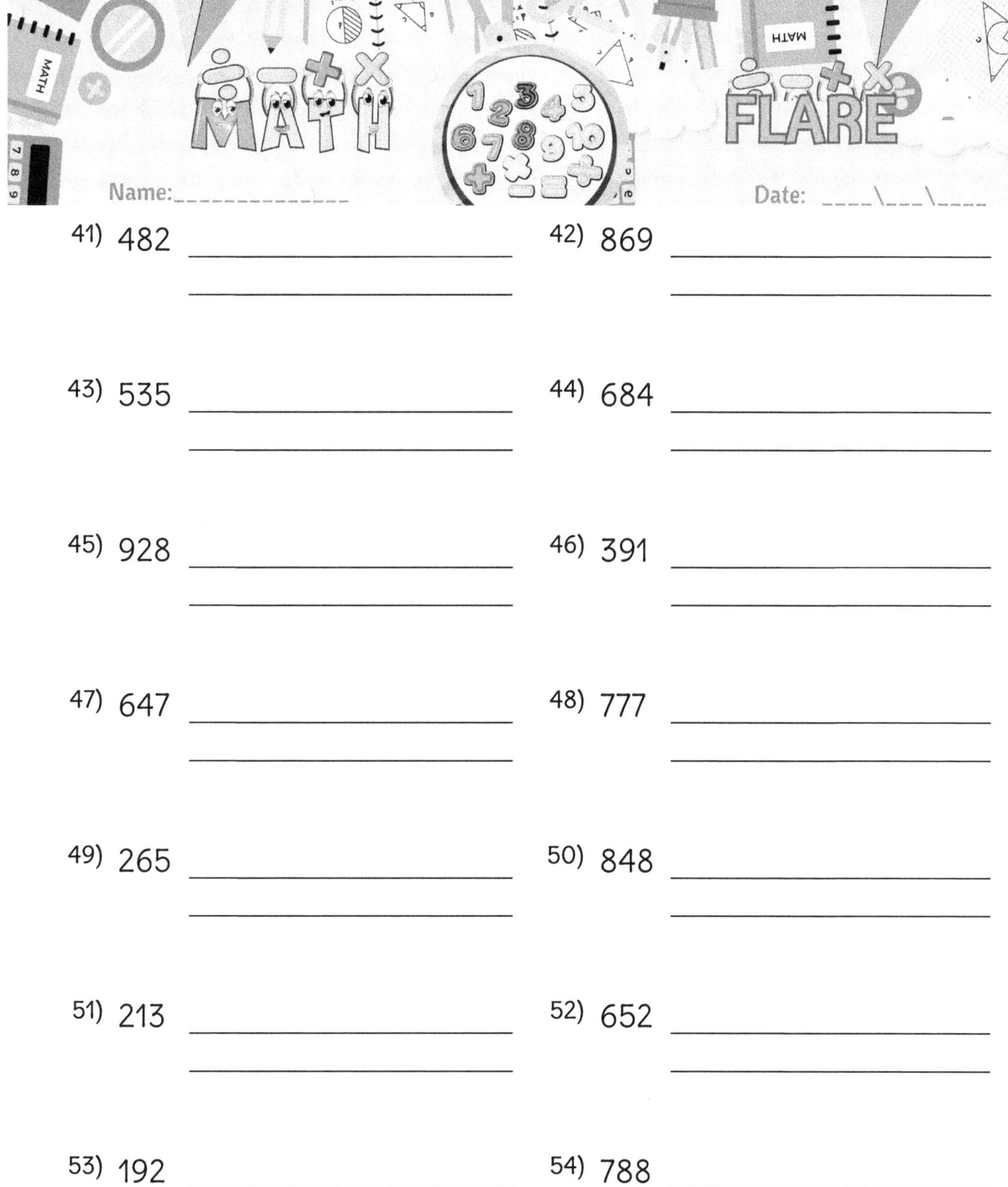

41) 482 _______________________
____

42) 869 _______________________
____

43) 535 _______________________
____

44) 684 _______________________
____

45) 928 _______________________
____

46) 391 _______________________
____

47) 647 _______________________
____

48) 777 _______________________
____

49) 265 _______________________
____

50) 848 _______________________
____

51) 213 _______________________
____

52) 652 _______________________
____

53) 192 _______________________
____

54) 788 _______________________
____

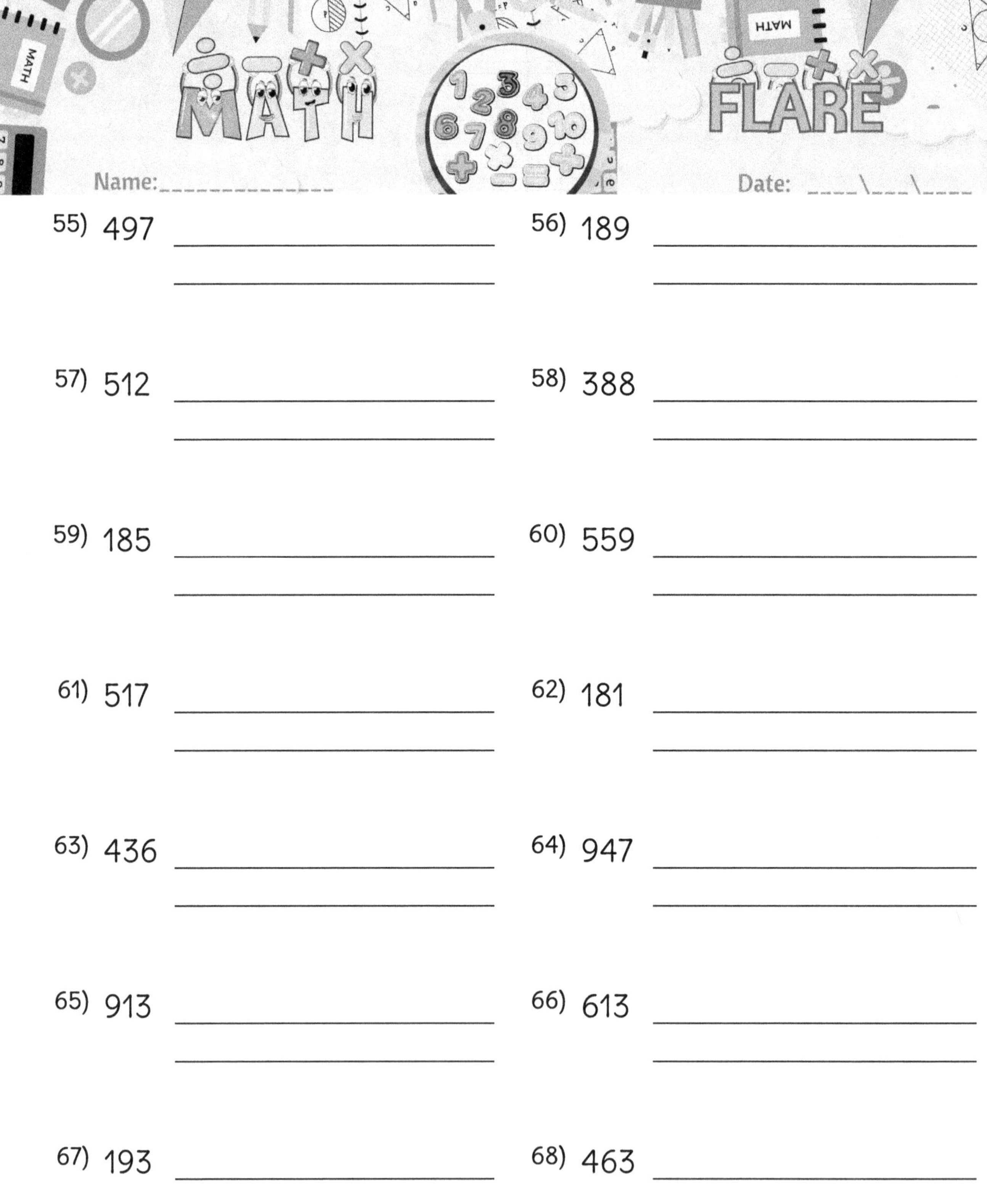

55) 497 ______________________

56) 189 ______________________

57) 512 ______________________

58) 388 ______________________

59) 185 ______________________

60) 559 ______________________

61) 517 ______________________

62) 181 ______________________

63) 436 ______________________

64) 947 ______________________

65) 913 ______________________

66) 613 ______________________

67) 193 ______________________

68) 463 ______________________

69) 504 _______________________

70) 670 _______________________

71) 696 _______________________

72) 194 _______________________

73) 761 _______________________

74) 961 _______________________

75) 690 _______________________

76) 948 _______________________

77) 801 _______________________

78) 753 _______________________

79) 959 _______________________

80) 214 _______________________

81) 228 _______________________

82) 393 _______________________

MathFlare - Math Workbook 2nd Grade

83) 573 _________________________
____

84) 215 _________________________
____

85) 659 _________________________
____

86) 720 _________________________
____

87) 138 _________________________
____

88) 899 _________________________
____

89) 936 _________________________
____

90) 595 _________________________
____

91) 275 _________________________
____

92) 923 _________________________
____

93) 354 _________________________
____

94) 810 _________________________
____

95) 101 _________________________
____

96) 737 _________________________
____

97) 141 _______________
____

98) 478 _______________
____

99) 35 _______________
____

100) 585 _______________
____

101) 802 _______________
____

102) 345 _______________
____

103) 543 _______________
____

104) 957 _______________
____

105) 998 _______________
____

106) 29 _______________
____

107) 536 _______________
____

108) 499 _______________
____

109) 564 _______________
____

110) 587 _______________
____

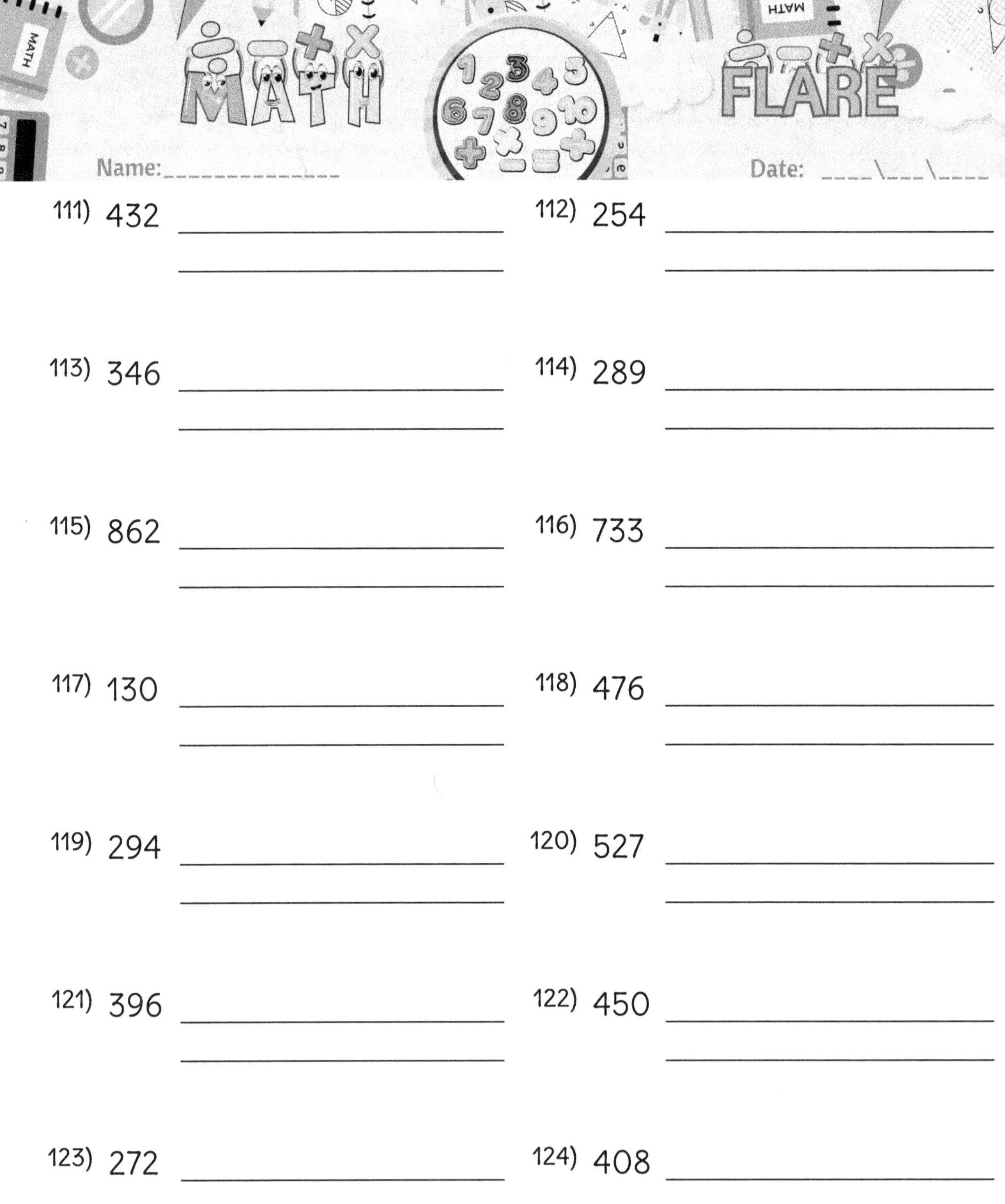

Name:___________________ Date: ____________

111) 432 ________________________

112) 254 ________________________

113) 346 ________________________

114) 289 ________________________

115) 862 ________________________

116) 733 ________________________

117) 130 ________________________

118) 476 ________________________

119) 294 ________________________

120) 527 ________________________

121) 396 ________________________

122) 450 ________________________

123) 272 ________________________

124) 408 ________________________

Name: _______________   Date: ____________

125) 152 _______________________
____

126) 590 _______________________
____

127) 212 _______________________
____

128) 661 _______________________
____

129) 276 _______________________
____

130) 925 _______________________
____

131) 629 _______________________
____

132) 426 _______________________
____

133) 49 _______________________
____

134) 31 _______________________
____

135) 259 _______________________
____

136) 692 _______________________
____

137) 603 _______________________
____

138) 401 _______________________
____

Understanding Time

1) 

9:35

2) 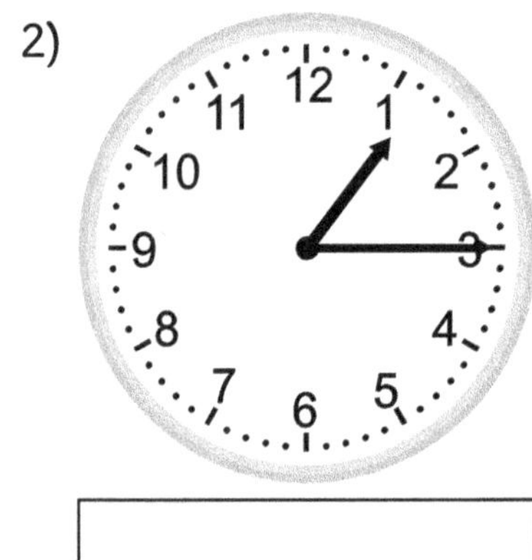

3) 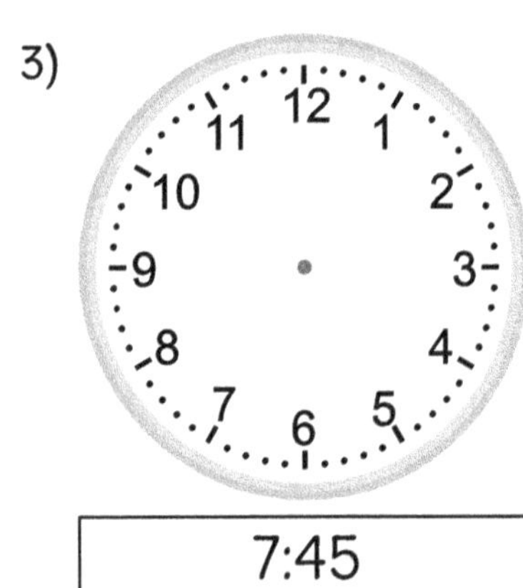

7:45

4) 

5) 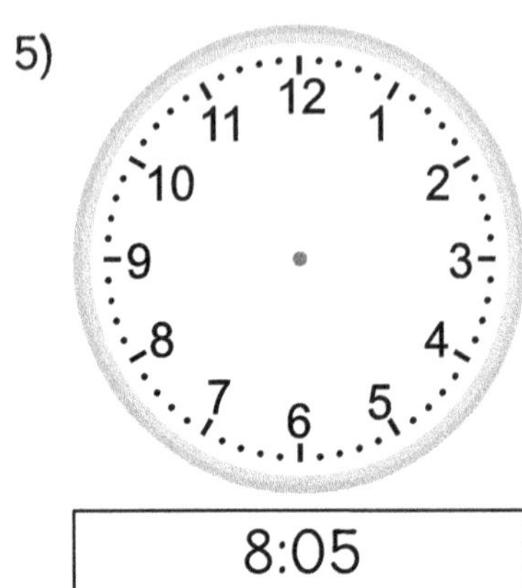

8:05

6) 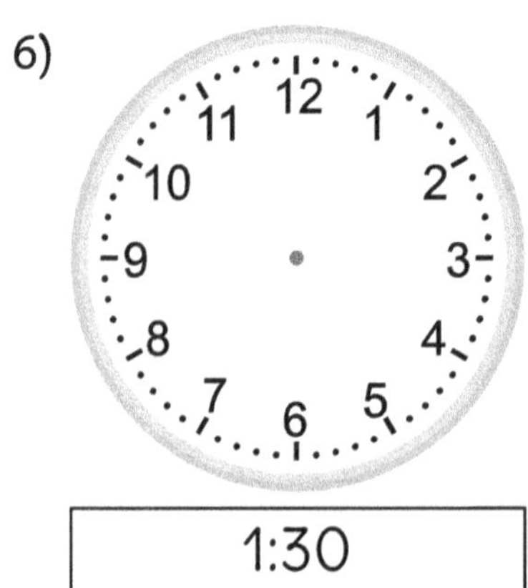

1:30

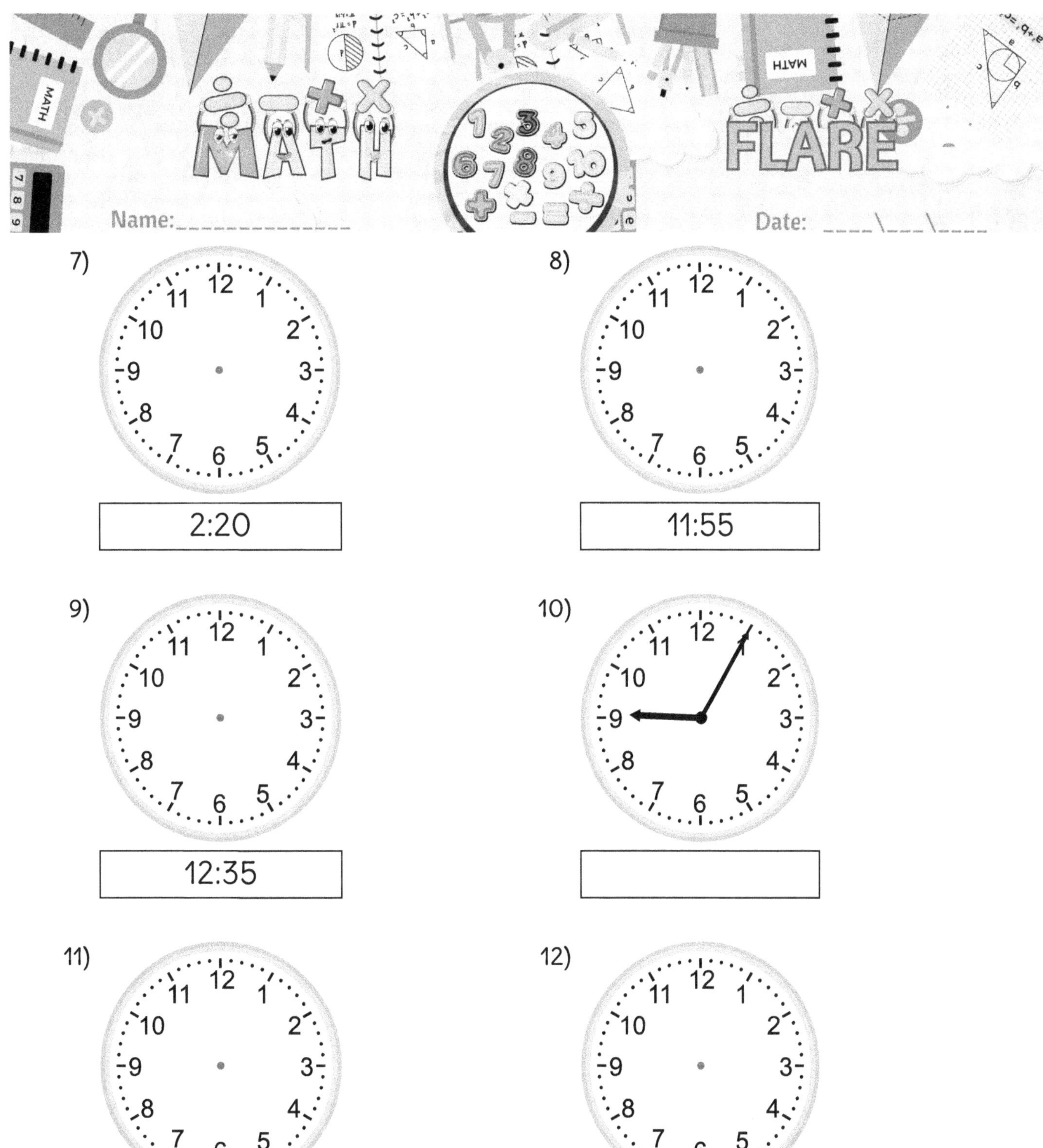

7)

2:20

8)

11:55

9)

12:35

10)

11)

3:45

12)

1:05

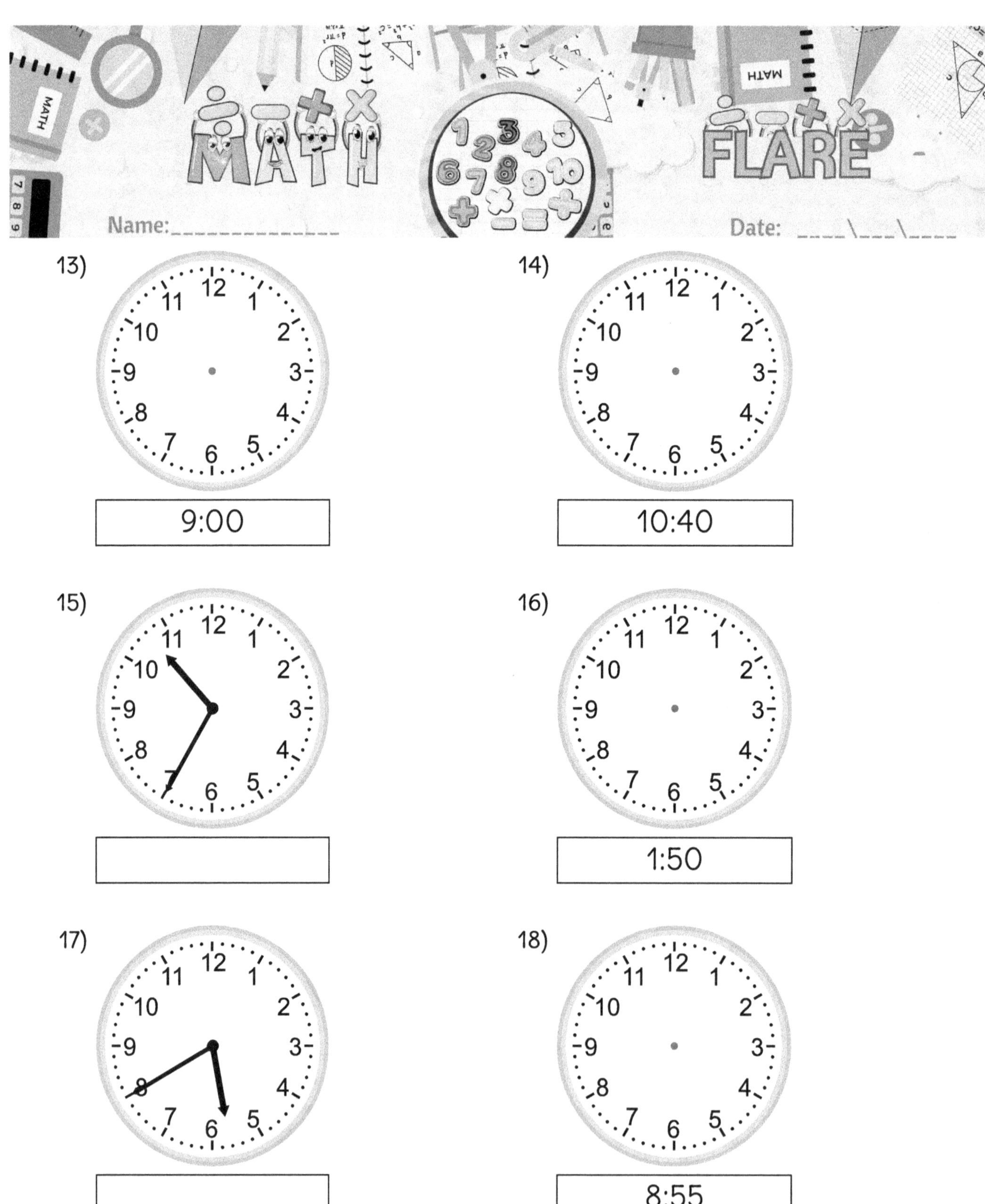

13)

9:00

14)

10:40

15)

16)

1:50

17)

18)

8:55

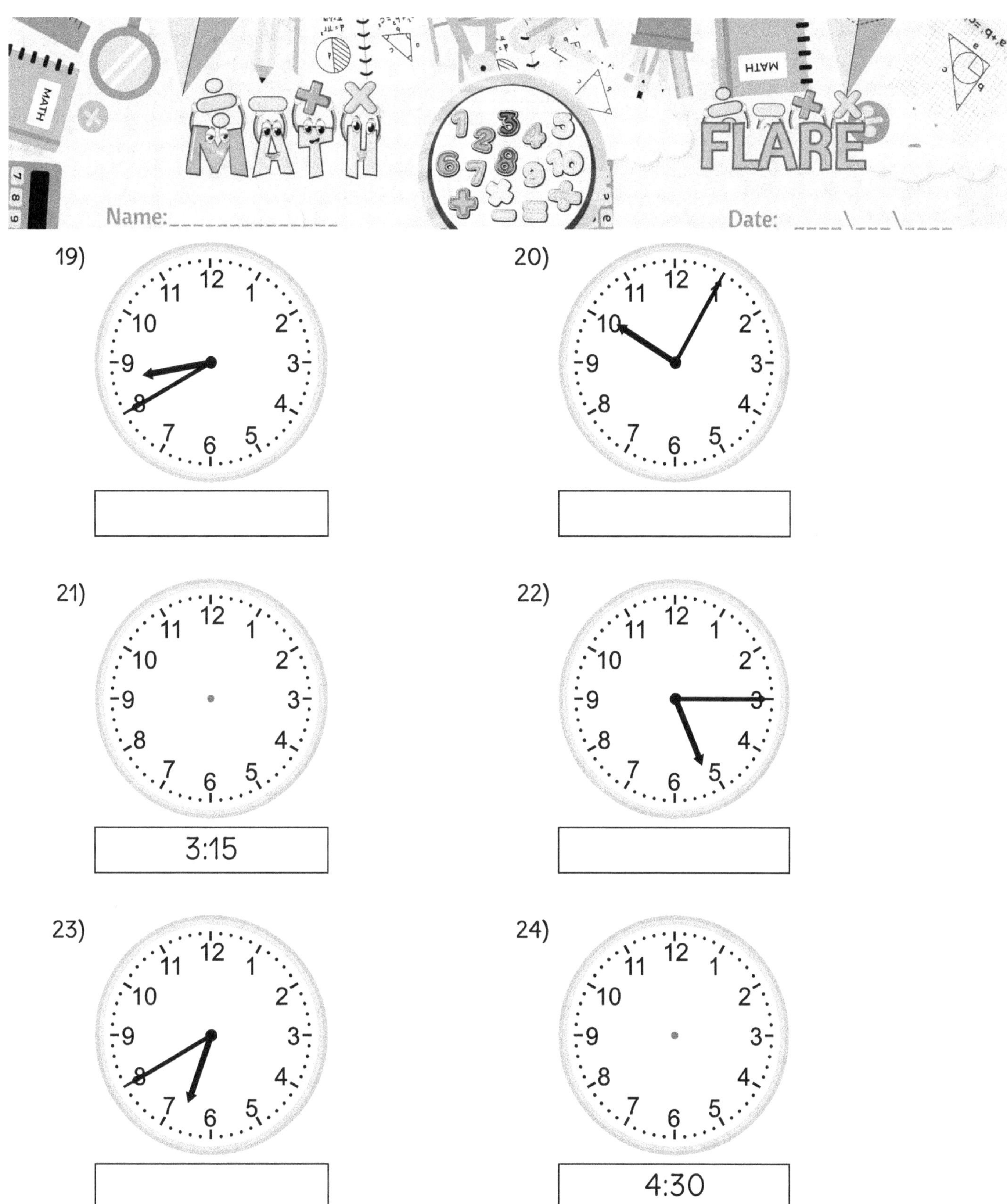

19)

20)

21)

3:15

22)

23)

24)

4:30

25)

26)

2:55

27)

28)

29)

30)

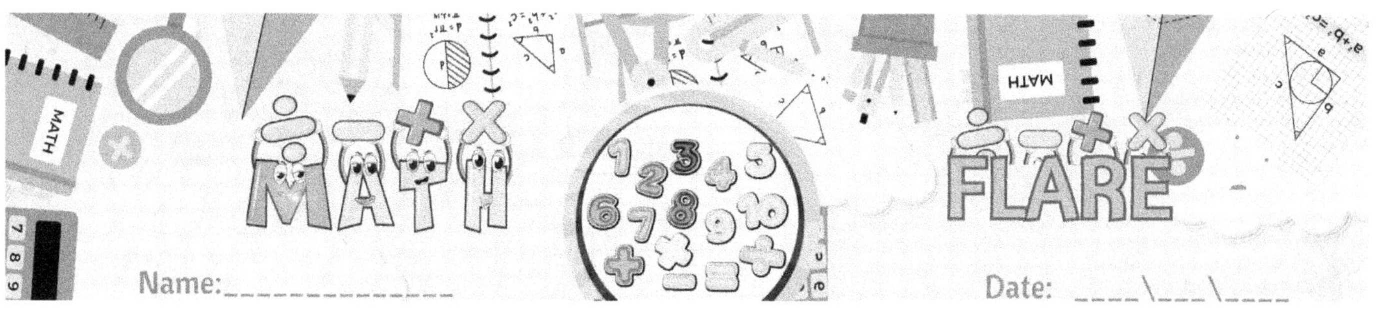

Measure the Rectangles

1)

4

5

2)

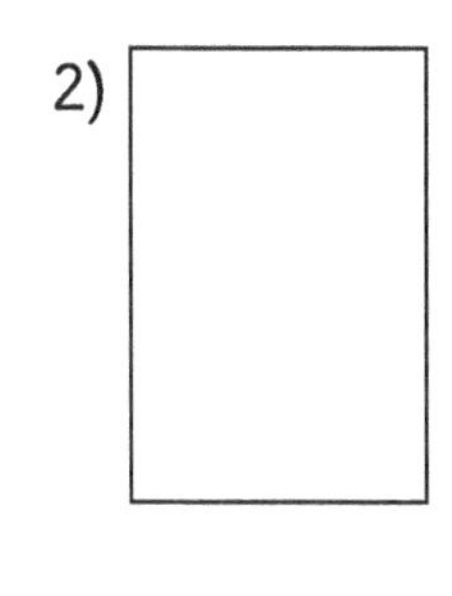

3)

4)

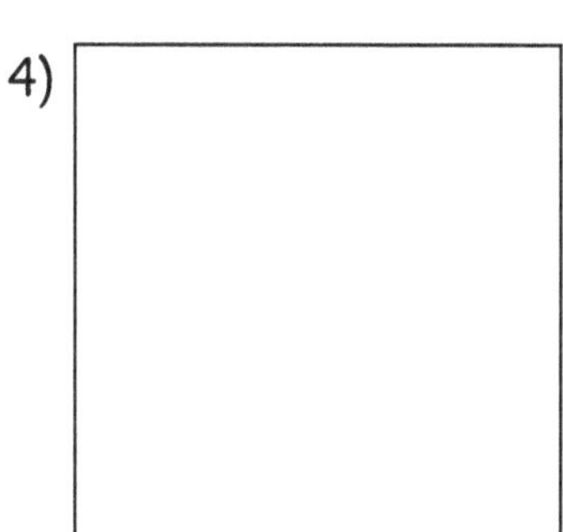

5)

6)

7)

8)

9)

10)

11)

12)

13)

14)

15)

16)

17)

18)

19)

20)

21)

22)

23)

24)

ANSWERS

Page 1:   Addition: 1 through 100

1. 167	2. 163	3. 62	4. 67	5. 91	6. 99	7. 47
8. 103	9. 155	10. 130	11. 28	12. 81	13. 129	14. 119
15. 101	16. 113	17. 149	18. 169	19. 106	20. 73	21. 109
22. 82	23. 77	24. 46	25. 93	26. 43	27. 79	28. 112
29. 62	30. 120	31. 106	32. 159	33. 180	34. 48	35. 68
36. 69	37. 100	38. 136	39. 97	40. 95	41. 171	42. 50
43. 97	44. 107	45. 142	46. 181	47. 72	48. 94	49. 126
50. 115	51. 94	52. 131	53. 92	54. 123	55. 171	56. 96
57. 101	58. 176	59. 78	60. 58	61. 109	62. 151	63. 81
64. 95	65. 139	66. 116	67. 72	68. 196	69. 92	70. 54
71. 71	72. 73	73. 85	74. 113	75. 150	76. 108	77. 74
78. 155	79. 103	80. 53	81. 85	82. 109	83. 155	84. 35
85. 95	86. 65	87. 121	88. 35	89. 108	90. 45	91. 125
92. 146	93. 96	94. 79	95. 117	96. 66	97. 135	98. 153
99. 117	100. 101	101. 108	102. 115	103. 147	104. 107	105. 156
106. 36	107. 92	108. 26	109. 74	110. 134	111. 91	112. 43
113. 96	114. 105	115. 96	116. 63	117. 76	118. 147	119. 116
120. 61	121. 41	122. 54	123. 117	124. 127	125. 98	126. 83
127. 24	128. 56	129. 51	130. 152	131. 31	132. 111	133. 161

134. 103	135. 87	136. 163	137. 190	138. 122	139. 75	140. 129
141. 119	142. 103	143. 100	144. 30	145. 46	146. 85	147. 49
148. 33	149. 63	150. 134	151. 85	152. 119	153. 113	154. 80
155. 119	156. 108	157. 143	158. 85	159. 6	160. 178	161. 155
162. 149	163. 109	164. 127	165. 141	166. 57	167. 116	168. 124
169. 84	170. 111	171. 117	172. 118	173. 59	174. 102	175. 174
176. 31	177. 99	178. 80	179. 87	180. 99	181. 82	182. 111
183. 82	184. 87	185. 120	186. 47	187. 179	188. 149	189. 52
190. 65	191. 118	192. 158	193. 61	194. 101	195. 117	196. 98

Page 11: Subtraction: 1 through 100

1. 1	2. 5	3. 14	4. 9	5. 9	6. 82	7. 12
8. 18	9. 19	10. 29	11. 18	12. 44	13. 20	14. 12
15. 19	16. 36	17. 34	18. 2	19. 65	20. 47	21. 4
22. 32	23. 15	24. 4	25. 50	26. 25	27. 7	28. 8
29. 43	30. 36	31. 34	32. 29	33. 66	34. 35	35. 40
36. 49	37. 94	38. 9	39. 45	40. 26	41. 28	42. 71
43. 83	44. 3	45. 59	46. 19	47. 39	48. 17	49. 6
50. 11	51. 7	52. 12	53. 33	54. 35	55. 53	56. 12
57. 5	58. 68	59. 28	60. 14	61. 30	62. 70	63. 36
64. 26	65. 17	66. 33	67. 12	68. 12	69. 19	70. 24
71. 13	72. 28	73. 10	74. 70	75. 5	76. 14	77. 30

78. 37	79. 12	80. 9	81. 44	82. 49	83. 9	84. 9
85. 10	86. 83	87. 13	88. 82	89. 3	90. 8	91. 31
92. 11	93. 10	94. 14	95. 30	96. 27	97. 25	98. 13
99. 49	100. 75	101. 64	102. 51	103. 56	104. 21	105. 7
106. 20	107. 30	108. 4	109. 52	110. 2	111. 20	112. 46
113. 19	114. 2	115. 4	116. 65	117. 2	118. 4	119. 14
120. 42	121. 2	122. 30	123. 3	124. 29	125. 19	126. 15
127. 66	128. 72	129. 50	130. 10	131. 20	132. 11	133. 1
134. 0	135. 8	136. 43	137. 36	138. 60	139. 19	140. 5
141. 16	142. 0	143. 48	144. 31	145. 1	146. 28	147. 9
148. 56	149. 79	150. 54	151. 21	152. 20	153. 23	154. 34
155. 12	156. 64	157. 37	158. 11	159. 2	160. 60	161. 60
162. 50	163. 17	164. 43	165. 29	166. 28	167. 67	168. 15
169. 63	170. 41	171. 1	172. 74	173. 7	174. 35	175. 75
176. 9	177. 12	178. 40	179. 14	180. 1	181. 69	182. 0
183. 23	184. 25	185. 32	186. 8	187. 14	188. 16	189. 6
190. 33	191. 74	192. 12	193. 6	194. 2	195. 6	196. 4

Page 21: Addition with Regrouping

1. 131	2. 130	3. 90	4. 100	5. 150	6. 122	7. 133
8. 121	9. 152	10. 70	11. 120	12. 120	13. 60	14. 110
15. 130	16. 125	17. 171	18. 110	19. 30	20. 110	21. 112

22. 184   23. 158   24. 126   25. 115   26. 142   27. 123   28. 113

29. 162   30. 153   31. 150   32. 124   33. 105   34. 111   35. 150

36. 144   37. 167   38. 130   39. 132   40. 111   41. 111   42. 133

43. 110   44. 63   45. 112   46. 70   47. 115   48. 190   49. 131

50. 162   51. 158   52. 111   53. 133   54. 142   55. 106   56. 135

57. 141   58. 131   59. 133   60. 141   61. 93   62. 146   63. 116

64. 120   65. 162   66. 121   67. 172   68. 121   69. 110   70. 182

71. 150   72. 126   73. 160   74. 110   75. 122   76. 22   77. 122

78. 130   79. 20   80. 134   81. 164   82. 33   83. 95   84. 116

85. 81   86. 140   87. 120   88. 112   89. 143   90. 18   91. 131

92. 185   93. 114   94. 171   95. 130   96. 61   97. 120   98. 121

99. 125   100. 121   101. 131   102. 142   103. 120   104. 60   105. 116

106. 115   107. 71   108. 30   109. 91   110. 63   111. 93   112. 140

113. 110   114. 130   115. 120   116. 142   117. 141   118. 132   119. 145

120. 110   121. 130   122. 141   123. 34   124. 154   125. 132   126. 118

127. 48   128. 172   129. 112   130. 132   131. 122   132. 132   133. 124

134. 124   135. 126   136. 130   137. 122   138. 112   139. 110   140. 157

141. 11   142. 133   143. 172   144. 121   145. 160   146. 60   147. 190

148. 123   149. 100   150. 163   151. 76   152. 130   153. 35   154. 153

155. 130   156. 132   157. 117   158. 140   159. 116   160. 113   161. 120

162. 152   163. 61   164. 151   165. 111   166. 112   167. 80   168. 132

169. 21   170. 170   171. 121   172. 112   173. 154   174. 110   175. 174

176. 120   177. 170   178. 125   179. 44   180. 82   181. 160   182. 120

183. 121   184. 180   185. 65   186. 40   187. 184   188. 134   189. 128

190. 160   191. 51   192. 120   193. 151   194. 160   195. 134   196. 121

197. 122   198. 114   199. 193   200. 161

Page 31: Subtraction with Regrouping

1. 19   2. 62   3. 31   4. 32   5. 8   6. 23   7. 19

8. 19   9. 3   10. 31   11. 11   12. 26   13. 49   14. 7

15. 12   16. 4   17. 27   18. 72   19. 1   20. 34   21. 15

22. 12   23. 23   24. 8   25. 66   26. 27   27. 7   28. 4

29. 49   30. 4   31. 18   32. 37   33. 9   34. 5   35. 5

36. 37   37. 37   38. 38   39. 3   40. 5   41. 27   42. 26

43. 4   44. 33   45. 4   46. 7   47. 3   48. 7   49. 4

50. 52   51. 4   52. 17   53. 8   54. 6   55. 57   56. 21

57. 3   58. 56   59. 31   60. 3   61. 12   62. 5   63. 74

64. 21   65. 69   66. 28   67. 21   68. 12   69. 38   70. 8

71. 33   72. 14   73. 27   74. 11   75. 27   76. 75   77. 17

78. 14   79. 35   80. 26   81. 61   82. 11   83. 6   84. 7

85. 67   86. 9   87. 67   88. 13   89. 48   90. 52   91. 14

92. 54   93. 29   94. 68   95. 13   96. 6   97. 82   98. 38

99. 25   100. 38   101. 13   102. 7   103. 15   104. 32   105. 44

106. 1	107. 22	108. 16	109. 58	110. 11	111. 46	112. 55
113. 9	114. 7	115. 3	116. 34	117. 77	118. 45	119. 11
120. 78	121. 39	122. 79	123. 33	124. 49	125. 47	126. 27
127. 85	128. 26	129. 35	130. 17	131. 33	132. 36	133. 13
134. 4	135. 19	136. 53	137. 18	138. 57	139. 6	140. 48
141. 9	142. 0	143. 16	144. 21	145. 0	146. 16	147. 84
148. 5	149. 16	150. 9	151. 14	152. 15	153. 29	154. 24
155. 51	156. 19	157. 68	158. 34	159. 37	160. 26	161. 17
162. 37	163. 7	164. 69	165. 5	166. 7	167. 22	168. 45
169. 38	170. 31	171. 3	172. 44	173. 36	174. 18	175. 8
176. 13	177. 46	178. 12	179. 6	180. 48	181. 36	182. 22
183. 17	184. 5	185. 42	186. 78	187. 5	188. 47	189. 6
190. 24	191. 3	192. 3	193. 77	194. 18	195. 3	196. 41

Page 41: Make 100

1. 7	2. 64	3. 3	4. 14	5. 2	6. 66	7. 99
8. 34	9. 85	10. 69	11. 96	12. 10	13. 78	14. 87
15. 82	16. 31	17. 93	18. 71	19. 43	20. 21	21. 95
22. 79	23. 92	24. 60	25. 18	26. 83	27. 97	28. 28
29. 63	30. 74	31. 17	32. 37	33. 67	34. 73	35. 32
36. 23	37. 6	38. 59	39. 35	40. 48	41. 20	42. 27
43. 5	44. 38	45. 4	46. 12	47. 61	48. 94	49. 81

50. 19   51. 75   52. 53   53. 45   54. 80   55. 54   56. 86

57. 57   58. 49   59. 25   60. 88   61. 47   62. 89   63. 39

64. 24   65. 56   66. 8   67. 68   68. 76   69. 16   70. 70

71. 22   72. 29   73. 33   74. 84   75. 50   76. 36   77. 52

78. 11   79. 42   80. 15   81. 77   82. 41   83. 90   84. 26

85. 72   86. 13   87. 46   88. 0   89. 62   90. 58   91. 30

92. 9   93. 55   94. 65   95. 98   96. 44   97. 91   98. 1

99. 51   100. 38   101. 40   102. 66   103. 62   104. 78   105. 79

106. 83

Page 47: Addition: Unknown Number

1. 37   2. 92   3. 75   4. 141   5. 8   6. 6   7. 43

8. 77   9. 88   10. 162   11. 94   12. 71   13. 99   14. 119

15. 67   16. 11   17. 147   18. 41   19. 135   20. 22   21. 7

22. 15   23. 122   24. 157   25. 82   26. 3   27. 83   28. 76

29. 40   30. 76   31. 2   32. 94   33. 92   34. 61   35. 11

36. 110   37. 44   38. 3   39. 119   40. 39   41. 67   42. 52

43. 23   44. 2   45. 42   46. 56   47. 78   48. 127   49. 127

50. 35   51. 35   52. 80   53. 84   54. 151   55. 16   56. 21

57. 17   58. 3   59. 68   60. 67   61. 54   62. 17   63. 45

64. 39   65. 46   66. 15   67. 13   68. 88   69. 22   70. 51

71. 77   72. 38   73. 75   74. 42   75. 92   76. 54   77. 154

78. 74	79. 90	80. 78	81. 46	82. 96	83. 163	84. 10
85. 129	86. 23	87. 18	88. 28	89. 80	90. 40	91. 81
92. 32	93. 104	94. 45	95. 49	96. 49	97. 73	98. 185
99. 19	100. 69	101. 42	102. 13	103. 93	104. 77	105. 83
106. 12	107. 31	108. 65	109. 84	110. 68	111. 65	112. 110
113. 130	114. 138	115. 36	116. 78	117. 61	118. 151	119. 72
120. 91	121. 167	122. 72	123. 117	124. 51	125. 29	126. 31
127. 47	128. 62	129. 36	130. 37	131. 60	132. 56	133. 79
134. 22	135. 14	136. 68	137. 50	138. 59	139. 70	140. 44
141. 160	142. 39	143. 85	144. 16	145. 87	146. 55	147. 33
148. 24	149. 44	150. 42	151. 5	152. 95	153. 36	154. 40
155. 23	156. 151	157. 20	158. 152	159. 76	160. 180	161. 33
162. 105	163. 78	164. 103	165. 84	166. 12	167. 96	168. 40
169. 60	170. 51	171. 20	172. 12	173. 36	174. 79	175. 105
176. 27	177. 56	178. 78	179. 55	180. 51	181. 74	182. 47
183. 41	184. 55	185. 157	186. 142	187. 44	188. 38	189. 8
190. 117	191. 60	192. 97	193. 36	194. 125	195. 62	196. 62

Page 58: Subtraction: Unknown Number

1. 20	2. 49	3. 39	4. 4	5. 23	6. 58	7. 10
8. 84	9. 15	10. 22	11. 41	12. 18	13. 38	14. 7
15. 61	16. 30	17. 15	18. 24	19. 100	20. 16	21. 14

22. 19	23. 73	24. 52	25. 29	26. 31	27. 92	28. 37
29. 56	30. 34	31. 28	32. 31	33. 35	34. 52	35. 36
36. 86	37. 16	38. 69	39. 68	40. 47	41. 6	42. 15
43. 45	44. 34	45. 67	46. 3	47. 3	48. 39	49. 19
50. 42	51. 31	52. 88	53. 14	54. 53	55. 28	56. 70
57. 27	58. 5	59. 10	60. 24	61. 50	62. 32	63. 82
64. 54	65. 61	66. 25	67. 27	68. 9	69. 51	70. 9
71. 7	72. 97	73. 13	74. 81	75. 5	76. 5	77. 4
78. 58	79. 73	80. 31	81. 26	82. 99	83. 43	84. 39
85. 6	86. 9	87. 23	88. 51	89. 13	90. 73	91. 55
92. 18	93. 26	94. 21	95. 60	96. 81	97. 75	98. 42
99. 36	100. 18	101. 1	102. 29	103. 7	104. 5	105. 43
106. 30	107. 28	108. 10	109. 40	110. 16	111. 18	112. 56
113. 37	114. 12	115. 76	116. 66	117. 24	118. 76	119. 51
120. 16	121. 40	122. 25	123. 42	124. 13	125. 38	126. 21
127. 40	128. 6	129. 28	130. 79	131. 18	132. 34	133. 2
134. 61	135. 57	136. 84	137. 57	138. 85	139. 67	140. 17
141. 68	142. 96	143. 2	144. 83	145. 38	146. 30	147. 34
148. 34	149. 7	150. 37	151. 68	152. 43	153. 31	154. 7
155. 31	156. 31	157. 29	158. 63	159. 3	160. 18	161. 9
162. 8	163. 14	164. 89	165. 89	166. 65	167. 64	168. 90

169. 31   170. 5   171. 2   172. 42   173. 13   174. 20   175. 89

176. 33   177. 4   178. 37   179. 5   180. 26   181. 12   182. 55

183. 42   184. 6   185. 69   186. 11   187. 22   188. 87   189. 5

190. 27   191. 11   192. 76   193. 8   194. 1   195. 2   196. 42

Page 69: Addition Word Problems

1. 27   2. 27   3. 22   4. 25   5. 15   6. 39   7. 20   8. 8

9. 30   10. 24   11. 15   12. 9   13. 3   14. 24   15. 28   16. 7

17. 20   18. 18   19. 32   20. 24   21. 18   22. 21   23. 22   24. 18

25. 19   26. 32   27. 11   28. 5   29. 29   30. 22   31. 34   32. 13

33. 27   34. 15   35. 11   36. 30   37. 18   38. 12   39. 27   40. 27

Page 79: Subtraction Word Problems

1. 2   2. 8   3. 5   4. 1   5. 5   6. 6   7. 3   8. 2   9. 1   10. 0

11. 5   12. 1   13. 1   14. 4   15. 1   16. 0   17. 2   18. 2   19. 0   20. 0

21. 3   22. 2   23. 4   24. 1   25. 4   26. 2   27. 3   28. 2   29. 0   30. 1

31. 2   32. 2   33. 4   34. 2   35. 1   36. 3   37. 5   38. 5   39. 1   40. 0

41. 0   42. 1   43. 1   44. 0

Page 90: Multiplication by 1

1. 6   2. 7   3. 1   4. 9   5. 8   6. 4   7. 2   8. 5   9. 3   10. 4

11. 5   12. 8   13. 9   14. 2   15. 6   16. 3   17. 7   18. 3   19. 2   20. 8

Page 91: Multiplication by 2

1. 12   2. 16   3. 14   4. 6   5. 8   6. 4   7. 10   8. 2   9. 18

10. 16   11. 8   12. 6   13. 14   14. 10   15. 12   16. 2   17. 18   18. 2

19. 2   20. 12

Page 92:   Multiplication by 3

1. 9   2. 21   3. 15   4. 12   5. 3   6. 24   7. 18   8. 27   9. 6

10. 6   11. 24   12. 12   13. 21   14. 15   15. 18   16. 3   17. 27   18. 3

19. 12   20. 21

Page 93:   Multiplication by 4

1. 32   2. 24   3. 28   4. 8   5. 20   6. 16   7. 4   8. 12   9. 36

10. 24   11. 20   12. 12   13. 8   14. 28   15. 32   16. 4   17. 36   18. 32

19. 8   20. 12

Page 94:   Multiplication by 5

1. 20   2. 30   3. 25   4. 10   5. 35   6. 15   7. 45   8. 5

9. 40   10. 40   11. 10   12. 20   13. 45   14. 15   15. 30   16. 5

17. 35   18. 40   19. 40   20. 25

Page 95:   Multiplication by 6

1. 36   2. 48   3. 12   4. 6   5. 18   6. 24   7. 30   8. 42   9. 54

10. 54   11. 12   12. 48   13. 24   14. 42   15. 18   16. 30   17. 6   18. 30

19. 12   20. 18

Page 96:   Multiplication by 7

1. 56   2. 49   3. 42   4. 14   5. 21   6. 7   7. 35   8. 28

9. 63   10. 56   11. 21   12. 42   13. 28   14. 63   15. 14   16. 7

17. 35   18. 49   19. 56   20. 28

Page 97:   Multiplication by 8

1. 16　　2. 64　　3. 48　　4. 8　　5. 56　　6. 32　　7. 40　　8. 24

9. 72　　10. 32　　11. 56　　12. 40　　13. 16　　14. 72　　15. 24　　16. 48

17. 8　　18. 16　　19. 16　　20. 32

Page 98:   Multiplication by 9

1. 27　　2. 63　　3. 72　　4. 18　　5. 36　　6. 45　　7. 54　　8. 81

9. 9　　10. 18　　11. 54　　12. 45　　13. 72　　14. 36　　15. 63　　16. 27

17. 9　　18. 36　　19. 27　　20. 45

Page 99:   Multiplication by 10

1. 90　　2. 80　　3. 60　　4. 10　　5. 70　　6. 50　　7. 30　　8. 40

9. 20　　10. 20　　11. 50　　12. 10　　13. 60　　14. 40　　15. 80　　16. 70

17. 30　　18. 90　　19. 40　　20. 60

Page 100:   Basic Multiplication

1. 16　　2. 48　　3. 4　　4. 5　　5. 6　　6. 20　　7. 50

8. 28　　9. 8　　10. 48　　11. 27　　12. 45　　13. 36　　14. 21

15. 24　　16. 12　　17. 63　　18. 80　　19. 10　　20. 6　　21. 90

22. 32　　23. 80　　24. 16　　25. 63　　26. 15　　27. 5　　28. 16

29. 40　　30. 32　　31. 12　　32. 18　　33. 30　　34. 56　　35. 50

36. 14　　37. 4　　38. 25　　39. 18　　40. 72　　41. 7　　42. 18

43. 56　　44. 12　　45. 72　　46. 10　　47. 3　　48. 30　　49. 1

50. 45　　51. 8　　52. 40　　53. 6　　54. 20　　55. 35　　56. 35

57. 42　　58. 9　　59. 10　　60. 42　　61. 14　　62. 15　　63. 4

64. 54   65. 36   66. 9   67. 7   68. 40   69. 30   70. 8

71. 12   72. 54   73. 30   74. 49   75. 18   76. 28   77. 10

78. 24   79. 90   80. 8   81. 81   82. 2   83. 64   84. 24

85. 36   86. 9   87. 27   88. 100   89. 20   90. 60   91. 2

92. 70   93. 24   94. 60   95. 3   96. 6   97. 20   98. 21

99. 70   100. 40

Page 105:   Commutative Property

1. 8   2. 7   3. 6   4. 5   5. 5   6. 3   7. 5   8. 6   9. 8

10. 5   11. 3   12. 5   13. 2   14. 7   15. 6   16. 7   17. 3   18. 10

19. 2   20. 1   21. 2   22. 2   23. 1   24. 6   25. 9   26. 2   27. 9

28. 2   29. 2   30. 5   31. 6   32. 9   33. 7   34. 3   35. 1   36. 9

37. 1   38. 3   39. 10   40. 8   41. 1   42. 8   43. 3   44. 6   45. 3

46. 4   47. 6   48. 1   49. 5   50. 5   51. 7   52. 2

Page 108:   Matching the answers.

1. a.B b.A c.D d.I e.G f.C g.J h.E i.F j.H

2. a.A b.E c.H d.I e.F f.C g.D h.J i.G j.B

3. a.E b.D c.B d.C e.I f.G g.H h.A i.F j.J

4. a.F b.C c.H d.I e.D f.B g.J h.G i.A j.E

5. a.G b.B c.D d.A e.I f.F g.E h.C i.J j.H

6. a.F b.J c.A d.C e.D f.H g.B h.G i.E j.I

7. a.I b.G c.A d.H e.C f.B g.J h.F i.D j.E

8. a.E b.J c.A d.C e.I f.G g.H h.F i.D j.B

9. a.H b.C c.A d.E e.F f.J g.G h.I i.D j.B

10. a.D b.B c.A d.E e.H f.J g.F h.C i.G j.I

Page 118: Place Value

1. 1 one	2. 9 hundreds	3. 3 hundreds
4. 8 tens	5. 4 tens	6. 5 tens
7. 8 tens	8. 5 hundreds	9. 7 hundreds
10. 3 ones	11. 0 tens	12. 2 tens
13. 3 hundreds	14. 4 ones	15. 7 hundreds
16. 7 ones	17. 1 one	18. 8 hundreds
19. 9 ones	20. 5 ones	21. 6 ones
22. 3 hundreds	23. 8 ones	24. 8 hundreds
25. 3 ones	26. 4 hundreds	27. 1 one
28. 5 ones	29. 6 ones	30. 6 ones
31. 2 tens	32. 0 ones	33. 9 ones
34. 0 tens	35. 3 hundreds	36. 5 tens
37. 9 tens	38. 3 hundreds	39. 2 tens
40. 5 hundreds	41. 7 hundreds	42. 5 hundreds
43. 1 one	44. 4 hundreds	45. 2 tens
46. 6 ones	47. 8 tens	48. 2 ones
49. 9 ones	50. 5 tens	51. 9 hundreds

52. 2 tens

53. 3 hundreds

54. 8 tens

55. 5 tens

56. 4 ones

57. 4 hundreds

58. 8 ones

59. 5 tens

60. 8 tens

61. 0 ones

62. 6 ones

63. 0 tens

64. 8 ones

65. 8 tens

66. 2 ones

67. 0 tens

68. 2 ones

69. 9 tens

70. 9 tens

71. 5 tens

72. 7 ones

73. 7 ones

74. 9 ones

75. 4 ones

76. 9 tens

77. 1 ten

78. 4 tens

79. 8 ones

80. 4 hundreds

81. 5 tens

82. 2 tens

83. 7 ones

84. 6 hundreds

85. 8 ones

86. 2 hundreds

87. 2 ones

88. 9 hundreds

89. 2 tens

90. 3 tens

91. 2 tens

92. 7 ones

93. 2 ones

94. 5 hundreds

95. 7 tens

96. 4 hundreds

97. 8 ones

98. 7 ones

99. 7 ones

100. 0 ones

101. 9 hundreds

102. 6 ones

103. 3 tens

104. 8 tens

105. 6 hundreds

106. 6 tens

107. 1 ten

108. 6 hundreds

109. 1 one

110. 8 ones

111. 8 tens

112. 8 tens

113. 6 hundreds

114. 3 tens

115. 5 ones   116. 8 tens   117. 9 ones

118. 4 hundreds   119. 1 one   120. 8 tens

121. 2 hundreds   122. 1 ten   123. 4 tens

124. 0 ones

Page 125:   Place Value: Expanded Notation

1. 26	2. 689	3. 33	4. 607	5. 231	6. 448
7. 663	8. 444	9. 617	10. 669	11. 908	12. 500
13. 779	14. 464	15. 159	16. 392	17. 368	18. 510
19. 622	20. 180	21. 196	22. 830	23. 471	24. 362
25. 248	26. 137	27. 635	28. 111	29. 560	30. 899
31. 829	32. 386	33. 564	34. 352	35. 438	36. 508
37. 32	38. 16	39. 241	40. 268	41. 907	42. 981
43. 580	44. 387	45. 626	46. 395	47. 39	48. 482
49. 11	50. 492	51. 728	52. 400	53. 644	54. 219
55. 671	56. 360	57. 96	58. 984	59. 29	60. 335
61. 58	62. 770	63. 81	64. 115	65. 216	66. 113
67. 720	68. 885	69. 337	70. 495	71. 382	72. 912
73. 290	74. 849	75. 891	76. 861	77. 70	78. 597
79. 628	80. 551	81. 408	82. 102	83. 985	84. 920
85. 158	86. 221	87. 837	88. 672	89. 257	90. 240
91. 573	92. 924	93. 810	94. 273	95. 412	96. 283

97. 319	98. 598	99. 674	100. 996	101. 347	102. 488
103. 355	104. 346	105. 328	106. 780	107. 499	108. 586
109. 915	110. 433	111. 706	112. 507	113. 363	114. 979
115. 130	116. 295	117. 955	118. 49	119. 665	120. 576
121. 127	122. 717	123. 925	124. 82	125. 590	126. 100
127. 787	128. 278	129. 877	130. 755	131. 498	132. 566
133. 811	134. 893	135. 174	136. 341	137. 807	138. 867

Page 135: Place Value: Expanded Notation

1. 4 hundreds + 1 ten + 8 ones

2. 4 hundreds + 4 tens + 8 ones

3. 4 hundreds + 1 ten + 3 ones

4. 1 hundred + 4 tens + 3 ones

5. 1 hundred + 1 ten + 7 ones

6. 3 hundreds + 2 tens + 8 ones

7. 8 hundreds + 1 ten + 9 ones

8. 5 hundreds + 5 tens

9. 9 ones

10. 4 hundreds + 2 tens + 2 ones

11. 2 hundreds + 2 tens + 1 one

12. 8 hundreds + 1 ten + 4 ones

13. 6 hundreds + 3 tens + 8 ones

14. 4 hundreds + 2 tens + 1 one

15. 2 hundreds + 4 tens + 7 ones

16. 2 hundreds + 8 tens + 1 one

17. 9 hundreds + 9 ones

18. 4 hundreds + 8 tens + 7 ones

19. 1 hundred + 2 tens + 9 ones

20. 1 hundred + 5 tens + 5 ones

21. 6 hundreds + 7 tens + 5 ones

22. 6 hundreds + 3 tens

23. 9 hundreds + 5 tens + 1 one

24. 2 hundreds + 2 tens + 5 ones

25. 6 hundreds + 3 tens + 2 ones

26. 7 hundreds + 2 tens + 9 ones

27. 1 hundred + 4 tens + 5 ones

28. 6 hundreds + 7 ones

29. 9 hundreds + 9 tens

30. 4 hundreds + 9 tens + 2 ones

31. 2 hundreds + 4 tens + 1 one

32. 7 hundreds + 8 tens + 5 ones

33. 8 hundreds + 6 tens + 7 ones

34. 8 hundreds + 5 tens

35. 5 hundreds + 8 ones

36. 6 hundreds + 3 tens + 4 ones

37. 8 tens + 8 ones

38. 4 hundreds + 4 tens + 7 ones

39. 9 hundreds + 8 tens + 2 ones

40. 4 hundreds + 5 tens + 9 ones

41. 4 hundreds + 8 tens + 2 ones

42. 8 hundreds + 6 tens + 9 ones

43. 5 hundreds + 3 tens + 5 ones

44. 6 hundreds + 8 tens + 4 ones

45. 9 hundreds + 2 tens + 8 ones

46. 3 hundreds + 9 tens + 1 one

47. 6 hundreds + 4 tens + 7 ones

48. 7 hundreds + 7 tens + 7 ones

49. 2 hundreds + 6 tens + 5 ones

50. 8 hundreds + 4 tens + 8 ones

51. 2 hundreds + 1 ten + 3 ones

52. 6 hundreds + 5 tens + 2 ones

53. 1 hundred + 9 tens + 2 ones

54. 7 hundreds + 8 tens + 8 ones

55. 4 hundreds + 9 tens + 7 ones

56. 1 hundred + 8 tens + 9 ones

57. 5 hundreds + 1 ten + 2 ones

58. 3 hundreds + 8 tens + 8 ones

59. 1 hundred + 8 tens + 5 ones

60. 5 hundreds + 5 tens + 9 ones

61. 5 hundreds + 1 ten + 7 ones

62. 1 hundred + 8 tens + 1 one

63. 4 hundreds + 3 tens + 6 ones

64. 9 hundreds + 4 tens + 7 ones

65. 9 hundreds + 1 ten + 3 ones

66. 6 hundreds + 1 ten + 3 ones

67. 1 hundred + 9 tens + 3 ones

68. 4 hundreds + 6 tens + 3 ones

69. 5 hundreds + 4 ones

70. 6 hundreds + 7 tens

71. 6 hundreds + 9 tens + 6 ones

72. 1 hundred + 9 tens + 4 ones

73. 7 hundreds + 6 tens + 1 one

74. 9 hundreds + 6 tens + 1 one

75. 6 hundreds + 9 tens

76. 9 hundreds + 4 tens + 8 ones

77. 8 hundreds + 1 one

78. 7 hundreds + 5 tens + 3 ones

79. 9 hundreds + 5 tens + 9 ones

80. 2 hundreds + 1 ten + 4 ones

81. 2 hundreds + 2 tens + 8 ones

82. 3 hundreds + 9 tens + 3 ones

83. 5 hundreds + 7 tens + 3 ones

84. 2 hundreds + 1 ten + 5 ones

85. 6 hundreds + 5 tens + 9 ones

86. 7 hundreds + 2 tens

87. 1 hundred + 3 tens + 8 ones

88. 8 hundreds + 9 tens + 9 ones

89. 9 hundreds + 3 tens + 6 ones

90. 5 hundreds + 9 tens + 5 ones

91. 2 hundreds + 7 tens + 5 ones

92. 9 hundreds + 2 tens + 3 ones

93. 3 hundreds + 5 tens + 4 ones

94. 8 hundreds + 1 ten

95. 1 hundred + 1 one

96. 7 hundreds + 3 tens + 7 ones

97. 1 hundred + 4 tens + 1 one

98. 4 hundreds + 7 tens + 8 ones

99. 3 tens + 5 ones

100. 5 hundreds + 8 tens + 5 ones

101. 8 hundreds + 2 ones

102. 3 hundreds + 4 tens + 5 ones

103. 5 hundreds + 4 tens + 3 ones

104. 9 hundreds + 5 tens + 7 ones

105. 9 hundreds + 9 tens + 8 ones

106. 2 tens + 9 ones

107. 5 hundreds + 3 tens + 6 ones

108. 4 hundreds + 9 tens + 9 ones

109. 5 hundreds + 6 tens + 4 ones

110. 5 hundreds + 8 tens + 7 ones

111. 4 hundreds + 3 tens + 2 ones

113. 3 hundreds + 4 tens + 6 ones

115. 8 hundreds + 6 tens + 2 ones

117. 1 hundred + 3 tens

119. 2 hundreds + 9 tens + 4 ones

121. 3 hundreds + 9 tens + 6 ones

123. 2 hundreds + 7 tens + 2 ones

125. 1 hundred + 5 tens + 2 ones

127. 2 hundreds + 1 ten + 2 ones

129. 2 hundreds + 7 tens + 6 ones

131. 6 hundreds + 2 tens + 9 ones

133. 4 tens + 9 ones

135. 2 hundreds + 5 tens + 9 ones

137. 6 hundreds + 3 ones

112. 2 hundreds + 5 tens + 4 ones

114. 2 hundreds + 8 tens + 9 ones

116. 7 hundreds + 3 tens + 3 ones

118. 4 hundreds + 7 tens + 6 ones

120. 5 hundreds + 2 tens + 7 ones

122. 4 hundreds + 5 tens

124. 4 hundreds + 8 ones

126. 5 hundreds + 9 tens

128. 6 hundreds + 6 tens + 1 one

130. 9 hundreds + 2 tens + 5 ones

132. 4 hundreds + 2 tens + 6 ones

134. 3 tens + 1 one

136. 6 hundreds + 9 tens + 2 ones

138. 4 hundreds + 1 one

Page 145: Understanding Time

1. 

9:35

2. 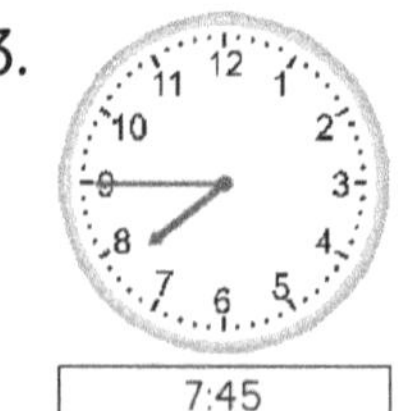

1:15

3. 

7:45

4.

3:20

5. 8:05	**6.** 1:30	**7.** 2:20	**8.** 11:55
9. 12:35	**10.** 9:05	**11.** 3:45	**12.** 1:05
13. 9:00	**14.** 10:40	**15.** 10:35	**16.** 1:50
17. 5:40	**18.** 8:55	**19.** 8:40	**20.** 10:05
21. 3:15	**22.** 5:15	**23.** 6:40	**24.** 4:30
25. 4:10	**26.** 2:55	**27.** 5:00	**28.** 10:25

29. 

6:55

30. 

12:25

Page 150: Measure the Rectangles

1. W=5 H=4
2. W=2 H=3
3. W=3 H=3
4. W=4 H=4

5. W=4 H=5
6. W=5 H=3
7. W=2 H=2
8. W=4 H=3

9. W=1 H=3
10. W=3 H=5
11. W=2 H=4
12. W=3 H=2

13. W=3 H=4
14. W=2 H=5
15. W=4 H=2
16. W=1 H=4

17. W=1 H=5
18. W=5 H=2
19. W=1 H=2
20. W=5 H=5

21. W=2 H=4
22. W=4 H=2
23. W=5 H=5
24. W=2 H=2